THEOLOGICAL ETHICS

JAMES SELLERS

THEOLOGICAL ETHICS

NEW YORK

THE MACMILLAN COMPANY

·

COLLIER-MACMILLAN LIMITED

LONDON

TO

C.M.S.

L.M.S.

CONTENTS

PREFACE

"THE NEW MORALITY" is a phrase we hear more and more. Sometimes it seems to mean mainly a new, relaxed attitude toward sex. Sometimes it means a new moral intensity among the young in our society, especially those concerned with racial justice, academic freedom, or world peace. At times it seems to mean something rather negative: revolt against yesterday's guidelines to behavior, or outright rejection of all hard-and-fast rules of conduct.

We need a new morality—every generation does. But before we can have it, we must think about a new ethics. And if we are going to base our new ethics and morality on the historic Christian faith, then we also need a new theology, or at least an approach to theology that takes most seriously the new world we live in.

In this book I have attempted to talk about a new ethics, yet one based on continued commitment to the Judaeo-Christian heritage. It should be said here that I have done little more than introduce the subject and point to some of the criteria that a reasonably comprehensive approach to Christian ethics ought to meet. And I have certainly not gone on to work out the details of a new morality; that is a different task. But I have sought to lay a basis for thinking about morality in our generation by outlining a new theological ethics.

Three assumptions that have gone into my thinking ought to be mentioned at the outset.

First, American theology must begin now to think more for itself, to hold up its end of the dialogue with European theology. This does not mean cutting off our theological roots, which lie deep in the Middle Ages, the Reformation, and the great modern

European traditions of liberalism and "neo-orthodoxy." While respecting and building on this Continental heritage, American theology is both able and obligated to speak more confidently now from its own distinctive stance.

This leads to the second assumption, which is that active human experience plays a larger role in the formation of theology than European religious thought has commonly allowed. Indeed, we cannot say what we mean by the very word "God" unless we ask what we mean by man. And this entails full appreciation for twentieth-century man, characterized by his initiative and ability as builder of cities, healer of bodies and souls, conqueror of the universe.

If we must take so seriously the reality of able, secular man, this does not mean we can omit a doctrine of God. Some contemporary theologians seem to have fallen into this trap in their insistence that a technological age, with its empirical bent and its self-sufficiency, must assume that "God is dead." But we can never define man adequately, no matter how able he becomes, without referring to God.

The central teaching of the Christian faith tells us that God and man are co-extensive realities. To define God, we point to men, and especially one man: Jesus Christ. But to define man, we point to God and say that man is that creature "like God" in initiative and outgoingness. And again, we point especially to the divinity of one man: Jesus Christ.

This sounds like circular reasoning, and that is what it is. It is the familiar theological circle, subscribed to in one form or another by Augustine, Calvin, and Tillich. God and man are interdependent realities; neither can be defined without the other.

My third assumption is that the Judaeo-Christian faith must now seek to contribute ethical insights to the world in a new way, less hampered by the ecclesiastical fractures and religious wars of the past. The ancient Catholic church has lately been setting the example for us on this score: it has shown a remarkable capacity to speak in love and fresh concern beyond the age-old barriers of hierarchy and dogma. Protestants must respond in kind. We live in an interdependent, pluralistic world. We must find a new theology that speaks to human ethical problems as such, and less to the polemical issues of the Reformation. That is one reason I have subjected the Protestant watchwords of justification by faith and *sola scriptura* to extensive criticism.

We live in an age in which man is demonstrating that he can do almost anything. This is as it should be, if he is truly created in God's image. But it also means he needs ethics more than ever. For the man who can do almost anything is more hard put to decide *what* to do than the man who cannot do very much in any case. Twentieth-century man has new power and unprecedented choices; hence his new responsibility to reflect on ethics.

JAMES SELLERS

Vanderbilt University

Part One

INTRODUCTION:

THE LOCI

I

THE ROLE OF CHRISTIAN ETHICS

TODAY

THE TWENTIETH CENTURY, we find it easy to say, has been a century of "retreat" for the Christian ethic. I suppose what we really have in mind is not so much Christian ethics as Christian *morality*. After all, we are usually echoing churchmen and politicians who dwell on the nation's "rapid moral decay," citing increased crime, drink, and divorce and darkly warning us that our detererioration may be at the point of no return. Or we may be thinking of drastically altered patterns of ordinary conduct and behavior—the casual acceptance of sexual intercourse among many college students, for example. All the same, it is not so evident that the changes have necessarily been in the direction of a retreat, on the whole. There is much to be said for the values of city life in this century in spite of the urban crime rate. Surely we must applaud the emancipation of women in our day—a phenomenon closely related to the new sexual freedom. Much (if not enough) has been done in this century to repair an infamous piece of American immorality: the injustice to which we have long subjected Negroes and other minority groups.

Aside from this objection to the easy saying, I think it side-tracks a more basic issue, the role of Christian ethics, properly so-called, in a day of change—not Christian morality, but Christian *ethics*. The difference between these terms, as I understand English usage, is now considerable. Etymologically, "ethics" and "morality" meant the same thing, the former coming from the Greek τὸ ἦθος, the latter from the Latin *mos* (pl. *mores*). Both originals meant "custom," "conventional conduct," "habitual way of action." Perhaps because the Greeks are supposed to have been

3

more philosophical, the Romans more practical, a difference in level of abstraction has crept in. Morality now has to do with day-to-day, actual conduct, human activity as it is guided and gauged by the most direct working rules of proper behavior. "Honesty is the best policy" is an example of one of these working rules; morality involves application of the rule to daily life.

When our living situation changes, we may need a new morality, one that translates our old responsibility into fresh rules of thumb. Yet morality, because it has to do with practical matters of application and is so closely tied to accepted patterns of conduct, is of little use at the task of standing off and appraising the need for revision. Morality is adapted to holding us to a given course of conduct, to going on with offering concrete guidelines, the same ones that worked before. *Ethics,* on the other hand, is a more systematic and comprehensive study of human actions, their significance, and our changing situation. It is a careful, reflective effort at knowledge which asks the meaning of human conduct in its setting and measures our conduct by some fundamental criterion of excellence or of ultimate value—its relation to our *duty* (or responsibility), or its place in leading us to *happiness* (or blessedness), to take the two most familiar criteria; or its "authenticity" in marking us as genuine human beings, to take the standard recently coined by existentialism.

Ethics, it can be seen, indirectly nourishes and sustains morality. "Moralities sooner or later outlive themselves, ethics never," the psychiatrist Erik Erikson argues in a notable essay on American youth, "morality is expendable only where ethics prevail."[1] It is the business of ethics to consider the great realities and changes in our life, and to lay out broad theoretical contributions toward testing and shaping morality, especially in times like ours of decisive social upheaval.[2]

Let us return to the saying, then, with which we began, that the twentieth century has been a time of retreat for Christian ethics. It is certainly true that today many Americans, including church people, have not responded to the dilemmas and challenges of our era by falling back on ethics, Christian or otherwise. Many among us, even in the churches, do not have the dimmest understanding of how to think ethically. Despite much talk of "renewal of the laity," and the wide publicizing of "study groups" on ethical issues, most of the actual fare in Protestant Christian education efforts has consisted of refurbished Victorian morality, often as seen and taught by businessmen's wives. Many church-men may indeed be "moral," that is, zealous in upholding certain practical guidelines to righteousness that have been handed down out of the recent past, but they are not *ethically* oriented, viz., equipped to reflect on human responsibility in the light of new demands on us, on the one hand, and of the theological principles of our heritage, on the other, which ought to furnish us criteria for testing our deeds. The apathy or hostility of numerous Chris-tian laymen to the civil rights struggle is the best example of this ethical vacuum. Another example is the tendency of some Ameri-cans to assess other nations in simplified moral terms as either "good" or "bad," "right" or "wrong"—again on the basis of a nineteenth-century moral code taken for granted, one that is rarely revised in the light of either the new facts of global life or of continued reflection from a thoughtful perspective—political, theological, or philosophical.

But this absence of ethical awareness is not just a failing of laymen in the churches and of ordinary citizens. It has all too often characterized twentieth-century leaders in all fields. Adolf Hitler, according to one of his biographers, Alan Bullock, com-bined a "technical virtuosity" with the grossness and ignorance of an ethical illiterate. For every Hitler, let us hope, there will al-ways be a Churchill, who was a profound political ethicist. Yet the course of twentieth-century politics, we may with reason fear, may not always be able to answer the Hitlers with leaders who think ethically, for the leaders of tomorrow are drawn from a citizenry less and less concerned with the formalities of ethics. Even where leaders are gifted with a sense of ethics, they are often inhibited by the ethical lag among their followers. A case in point is the white clergy in the South, a group which in becoming more professionally and theologically mature has found itself more and more estranged from rank-and-file communicants. Vari-ous studies converge on the conclusion that laymen cling to regional perspectives or provincial interests while their pastors show intensified concern "with truths applicable to all men in all conditions."[3]

Despite the absence of ethical thinking in some of the places where it is needed today, there are hopeful signs. If it is true that Americans remain concerned more with practical morality, and often outmoded varieties of it, than with ethics as such, ethical study is being taken more seriously in some sectors of the society. Since World War II many colleges have strengthened their undergraduate courses in religion and philosophy and have expanded their offerings in ethics. Theological seminaries have been strengthening their curricula in Christian ethics and social ethics for a generation. Courses in ethics are now taught in medical schools and law schools, and on university campuses there is much interdisciplinary discussion of ethics as related to the professions and to responsible citizenship. According to one psychiatrist, the unrest exhibited by college students in the last few years points to a renewed ethical consciousness and a new critical attitude toward the American social order and official foreign policy. Not long after student demonstrations had shaken the Berkeley campus, a University of California faculty committee issued a report suggesting that a "moral revolution of the young" is taking place. "Rather than aiming to be successful in an achievement-oriented society," the chairman commented, the students "want to be moral men in a moral society."[4]

The real problem that faces us today is not the breakdown of morality or the retreat of Christian ethics. It is, rather, the gap in America between morality and ethics. Those who protest their concern for morality the most vehemently are often the least capable of true ethical reflection. At the same time, the well educated and professional classes, who may show a high sense of ethical responsibility on public and political matters, may be less interested in personal morality,[5] or in retaining those parts of established morality that still strengthen us. What is needed is a new sense of the interdependence between ethics and morality, of course. What is needed is a recognition of the moral rebuilding based on ethical reflection that is brought on us by our times. Our situation today, in the complex and frustrating situations we have to face, includes the experiences of guilt and failure, the collapse, as the Catholic theologian Karl Rahner puts it, of our "good will to know and to do the right thing."[6] But this situation, so threatening on its face, is an invitation for us to participate in the resurgence of Christian ethics.

II

ETHICAL THINKING AMONG

THEOLOGIANS

WHEN WE TURN for help to recent ethical reflection among Protestant theologians, we find some hopeful signs—and some disturbing ones. First, the twentieth century represents a solid restoration of the study of theology, stemming from the revival of interest in biblical revelation set off by Karl Barth and other European theologians about the time of World War I. This theological movement—"dialectical theology" or "neo-orthodoxy"—while now past its peak has had a most constructive effect on Christian-ethical reflection by indicating the cruciality of a theological foundation or starting point. A classic, creative example of neo-orthodox theology as the basis of Christian ethics is Emil Brunner's *The Divine Imperative*—in many ways a masterpiece in which a fundamental motif of the Reformation, justification by faith, is treated systematically as the fountainhead of ethical reflection.[7]

Yet neo-orthodoxy, generally speaking, produced no great fever to think systematically or comprehensively. Such theologians as Barth at first resisted the whole idea of "systematic" thinking (though his own *Dogmatics* is more profoundly systematic than he cares to admit). Barth holds that human criteria of comprehensiveness must take second place to the positive hearing of the Word of God. He also denies the propriety of isolating "ethics" from theology proper, holding that this step might dissever ethical reflection from the source out of which it lives: God's word and deed. Besides, theologians of this period were widely influenced by Søren Kierkegaard, whose existentialist followers for a time almost dominated the Protestant theological establishment.

8

This meant widespread suspicion of comprehensive thinking, principles, and theories. Ethics was supposed to stress, rather, concrete responsibilities, the urgency of "decision" and "witness," the posture of openness to fresh personal reality and to subjectively apprehended truth. The greatest of American Christian-ethical thinkers of this period was Reinhold Niebuhr, and with him we find an indigenous American outlook—pragmatism—reinforcing the existentialist, anti-systematic features of dialectical theology. Not even Niebuhr's most careful and reflective work—*The Nature and Destiny of Man*—is truly systematic and comprehensive.[8]

The upshot is that neo-orthodoxy rightly stressed the *importance* of ethical thinking, as a pursuit of theology, but did little toward going about it systematically and hence did nothing to stem the growing cleavage between morality and ethics described above.

If this older twentieth-century theological movement is still vastly influential in contemporary circles, we can nevertheless observe that it is rapidly being surpassed. There is a distinct changing of the guard in contemporary theology, with younger thinkers beholden to, but not reproducers of, neo-orthodoxy coming to notice.

The first point we notice about these younger theologians is their skepticism of rounded-off, satisfying theological thinking. They are acutely aware of the difficulties of believing in God in the twentieth century, and if (1) "God is dead," then (2) theology in its dogmatic form as reflection about him is also a pretty futile venture. In the thought of one of the most outspoken of these theologians, Thomas J. J. Altizer, we find both of these skeptical themes. "No longer can the idea of God bring us security in the world; no longer can the Christian know God as the Absolute who is the source of all meaning, order, and reality in the world." If that is the case, then we are not surprised to find that "dogmatic theology proper has virtually died in recent years," and such an apparently magnificent achievement as Barth's *Dogmatics* in reality "performs the invaluable service of demonstrating the archaic nature of the orthodox theological tradition, for perhaps nowhere else may one encounter so many meaningless sentences."[9]

On the one hand, then, the prospects that we will get help in rethinking Christian ethics from these newer theologians seem exceedingly dim. In actuality, these notes of skepticism are only an intensification of tendencies already at work in neo-orthodoxy. The younger, daring Karl Barth of World War I vintage never exactly wrote about the death of God, but he did denounce "religion" and all human attempts to relax securely while believing in a comfortable God. He also objected to efforts to capture the essence of the Christian God in systematic form—though Altizer thinks that is just what the more mature Barth, the professor of theology, has spent his career doing. At all events, these younger theologians, especially in America, have not departed as much from neo-orthodoxy as they think, and seem bent on retaining its anti-metaphysical, anti-systematic bias, as well as the emphasis upon Christology which often comes at the expense of a sound, comprehensive doctrine of creation.

The last notable theologian of neo-orthodoxy was a younger Lutheran executed by the Nazis in 1945, Dietrich Bonhoeffer. Bonhoeffer's final speculations led him to put great stress on the integrity of "secular" life, but this was not as serious a break with Barth and earlier neo-orthodoxy as has been claimed. For Bonhoeffer stressed the "secular" at the expense of religious, metaphysical thinking. God may be imagined to speak directly to secular man, he suggests, rather than through religious systems, and this secular man is one who understands reality in terms of empirical phenomena. Thus revelation comes not through principles, systems, and theories, but through the concrete deeds and words of the man Jesus. But Barth himself had already said much the same thing. To be sure, American followers of Bonhoeffer have now gone further: Paul Van Buren insists that the word "God" itself is an artifact of metaphysical, religious thinking, and he attempts to transmute theological language into a kind of quasi-empirical description of the distinctive qualities of the man Jesus ("contagious freedom" which may be shared by others). But not even Van Buren's attempt to take the meaning of the

Gospel in "secular terms," i.e., empirically in some sense, is so far from classical neo-orthodoxy. Transcendence does not refer to the extraterrestrial existence of God, but to the claim of the neighbor upon us, which is seen *par excellence* in the Gospel, "the story of the man who was free for others even to the point of death, and whose freedom has been contagious." As the New Testament writers recommend, we must therefore rivet our attention upon the man Jesus, for "questions about 'God' will receive their only useful answer in the form and history of that man."[10] Yet all this is a favorite theme of Karl Barth himself, upon whom both Van Buren and Bonhoeffer are dependent.

Still there is a difference, and this is seen in the refreshing atmosphere of positive affirmation of the secular among these younger theologians. They are, in fact, a new generation of cultured despisers of religion. They continue to sound like Barthians and old-fashioned existentialists when they reject "structural pretensions" for theology and ethics and publicize the inadequacy of human minds and spirits "to face the terror both of the world and of God" (William Hamilton). For all that, they do manifest a healthy openness to the temporal, the spatial, the active reality of "empirical" life. This orientation, in the end, will turn out to be a boon to ethical reflection. If the meaning of the Easter story and the import of the Gospel are not to be discovered in metaphysical and religious explanation, they are nonetheless to be found "in the areas of the historical and the ethical" (Van Buren). If "the form and structure of a new essence of Christianity will be fragmentary," even a fragmentary Christian vision can give rise to "a distinctive style of life," "a Christian ethic" (Hamilton).[11] If there are doubts in this generation about comprehensive thinking, there is still much interested investigation of ways to replace, finally, the cultic church of the Middle Ages and the confessional church of the Reformation with a "reflecting and communicating" church, for which "proclamation takes the form of theological reflection in a secularized world" (Gibson Winter).[12] We cannot simply say, as many existentialists and theologians of the past generation did, that to consider man's spiritual pilgrimage has nothing to do with his biological and historical evolution.[13] These two sides of his being—spiritual and physical—have everything to do with each other; they are part of the one monopolar reality of man on the way to fuller manhood. It is the business of Christian ethics to reflect on this journey.

In contemporary Christian ethics, both European and American, there is already something of a recent set of starts toward systematic thinking. In this country, the treatises of Paul Ramsey, George Thomas, and E. C. Gardner represent, in one way or another, the implementation of reflective, comprehensive approaches to Christian ethics. Ramsey, for example, chooses the title of his book, *Basic Christian Ethics*, to point to the fact that fundamental questions are dealt with in it. Yet I do not believe Ramsey has fully succeeded in systematic thought according to the conception of completeness which I shall be insisting on in the next chapter. Indeed, he himself points to incompleteness: "No complete analysis of special social problems is attempted," he says. "This is not basic."[14]

The time has come, I believe, for a further effort at systematic thought in Christian ethics, one which can participate in the theological revisions which are modifying neo-orthodoxy, and one which can attempt to make contact with the moral dilemmas of American society in an effort to encourage ethical thinking. In any case, the "systematic approach" that I will suggest cannot be thought of in the purely rational or idealist sense of "system" which might have been possible before neo-orthodoxy and existentialism. I can speak, because of these elements in my theological heritage, only of a systematic approach that is based upon some kind of concrete, "historical" reflection—that is the way theological "system" has meaning for me. In the section that follows, then, I have called upon my own reading of the history of theology to furnish the ingredients, the raw material, of a systematic approach to Christian ethics.

III

THE LOCI OF A

CHRISTIAN-ETHICAL SYSTEM

FEW AGES HAVE PRODUCED systems of theological ethics that satisfy what we are capable of thinking of today as the minimum standards of systematic completeness. Until the nineteenth century, rather, ethical writings in Christian thought tended to be specializations in one or two of the specific areas or "loci"[15] which now occur to us. The ancient church, for example, even in its highest ethical genius, Augustine, conceived Christian ethics in no comprehensive, unified way. Augustine was indeed successful in propounding a truly theological motif for ethics (*caritas*) and in elaborating a theory of virtue based upon it (i.e., in his redefining the classical virtues in terms of the theological reality of love). Yet when faced with implementing his theory of virtue in the practical problems of the Christian life, he often lapses into the *ad hoc* consideration of cases and sometimes fills in the void between theory and application by moralistic homily.[16]

With the renovation of the meaning of faith that came in the Reformation, especially at the hands of Martin Luther, Christian ethics received anew a powerful theological basis. Protestantism has typically, in theory at least, founded ethics upon faith rather than upon the natural virtues on the one hand, as with secular ethics, or upon love on the other, as with Catholicism. This characteristic flows in large part from Luther, for no one is more convincing than he at the description of the untroubled vocation of the willing believer—who loves and finds his way to God out of the prior reality of his faith in Christ. Yet for all his gift at writing for the "simple layman" about the fundamental importance of justification by faith for the ethical life, for all his communicative skill in producing graphic pictures of various aspects of the Christian calling, Luther does not believe in laying out a comprehensive theory of virtue. Moreover, he is reluctant to ask, as Catholics and Protestant sect groups have not been, how the theological reality of faith may be recognized in human conduct when it comes true, hits home, is realized. This is seen in his refusal to treat carefully the subject of sanctification, taking it for granted, as he does, that the life of faith will be sanctified enough without our asking anxious questions about it. In Luther's mind, says Troeltsch, "the attainment of a fundamental religious position was the genuine moral imperative," and that, once achieved, made everything else seem "comparatively indifferent and obvious."[17]

That this additional aspect of Christian ethics—realization or *fulfillment* of faith in terms of life—must be treated responsibly by evangelical theologians is argued in the works of figures as diverse as John Wesley and Jonathan Edwards, both representing the eighteenth-century rounding off of the Reformation. The latter in particular excels at furnishing his ethics with a criteriology of realization, especially in his classic *Religious Affections*. And in Edwards' case at least, adequacy at the locus of "realization" (or fulfillment) does not rob him of depth at the original point of concern, that of the underlying theological motif. Edwards' doctrine of benevolence to being, explicated in *The Nature of True Virtue*, in effect restates and more definitely ethicizes the Reformation *leitmotif* of justification by faith.

It is a commonplace among theologians of neo-orthodox vintage that such ethically and politically minded religionists as Thomas Jefferson are "hardly worth reading." But this view, I have discovered, is part and parcel of that recent tendency in theology, noted in the foregoing chapter, to think "existentially" rather than comprehensively about Christian ethics. Jefferson, no Trinitarian, does fail us miserably at one locus—the same point at which Augustine, Luther, Jonathan Edwards, and Karl Barth can be relied on, viz., the offering of a profound theological stance for ethics. When he is thinking of this aspect, Jefferson casually disclaims the need of any revelational basis for ethics. He proposes what seems to theologians an inadequate stance—that "utility" or societal happiness is the best standard of excellence for human conduct, as opposed to, say, *sola fide*. Here he shows his affinity for the human exuberance of the Enlightenment and young America. Men are now to express themselves as creatures of God not by any kind of limp dependence upon the supernatural, but rather in their capacities, endowed them by God, of living justly, uprightly, and humanely. In other words, Jefferson, along with the Levellers of the English Revolution, the American Social Gospel, and the Negro non-violent movement of our own day, offers us *a further locus* of ethical thinking, one which is all too easily overlooked by those who list too noticeably toward dogmatics. Religious faith and its associated values must be converted, or at least convertible, into the coin of political and social activity. "I doubt whether the people of this country would suffer an execution for heresy, or a three years' imprisonment for not comprehending the mysteries of the Trinity," Jefferson says in his early *Notes on Virginia,* indicating his skepticism of "pure" theology. But something more must be said for "applied" theology, for he asks: "Can the liberties of a nation be thought secure when we have removed their only firm basis, a conviction in the minds of the people that these liberties are the gift of God?" There is no contradiction here; Jefferson sees political salvation as coming from the Creator—but it must be accepted, acted on, *appropriated*, rather than held as a mere belief. The most significant word in the Jeffersonian political lexicon is "rights," says Daniel J. Boorstin. It was always a watchword about man's ethical responsibility. Yet it was also, at the same time, a translation into temporal action of a divine gift: "The word 'right' was always a signpost pointing back to the divine plan of the Creation."[18]

Jefferson doubtless exaggerates the role of translation of the religious stance into political and social implementation. Worship, according to the New Testament (e.g., the act of pouring costly oil on Jesus' head), properly is a concomitant to ethics (e.g., spending the money for the poor—John 12:1-8). Yet a systematic theological ethics, we can now see, must provide just this complementarity between theological stance and social-political implementation. Hence we will do well to listen to Thomas Jefferson, with whom the abstraction that God creates man in his image comes to powerful expression in the political conception of the rights of man. Nor must we too narrowly interpret the content of the locus of action and think of it only as "political" action or efforts at "social justice." The task described by this locus of Christian-ethical thought is to find ways of enacting the theological stance, of putting it into reality among groups and selves. In the social realm this does indeed entail the uses of politics, law-making, and the civil phenomena of justice and equality. But the locus itself must not be restricted to any particular kinds of action, at least in advance, and the locus extends to the personal life as well as to the political-social realm.

It remained for the late nineteenth-century ethicists of German religious liberalism, influenced by Kant and Schleiermacher, to furnish the clue for another locus, namely in their conception of Christian-ethical knowledge as a viable, consistent, comprehensive theory of virtue capable of standing upon its own ground. Especially with Wilhelm Herrmann was the independence of ethical thought from dogmatic authority forcefully stated:[19]

> An ethics that means to be called "Christian" must insist in the name of religion as well as the name of science upon the independence [Selbständigkeit] of moral knowledge. . . . We are not to trace ethical thought back to something else in order to certify its truth. It is to be intelligible as truth through its own substance.

Herrmann's argument rests visibly upon Kant's notion that ethical authenticity is gained only when moral knowledge is not based upon natural inclination but rather is founded upon whole-hearted willingness. Thus for Herrmann the self-sustaining character of Christian ethics is a proposition that not only defines the status of ethics as a science but also describes the proper ethical outlook for personal morality. Morality is a mode of conduct [Verhalten] in which "human life surpasses its nature-bound way and is to acquire another style of life through its own activity. . . . This self-directed activity we call 'will.'" This ethical system visualizes the Christian faith as source of strength for person and community, but not necessarily as source of knowledge of what to do. "Christians are indeed utterly deluded," Herrmann stoutly insists, "if they hold themselves called and bound to appropriate and repeat with firm resolution as their own opinions all that such a man as Paul has said." The beginning of true morality lies in our beginning to live out of our own initiative, following no desires which enslave, but obeying only what we ourselves acknowledge as unconditionally necessary.[20] Hence the question of the independence of ethical thought shows itself as a question about the provenance of knowledge influential upon ethical decision, and is therefore closely related to the conventional dogmatic question of the relation between revelation and reason. In subsequent discussion, we will treat this locus under the heading of the problem of *wisdom* for Christian ethics: its sources, both sacred and secular, and the relations among them.[21]

We can discern, then, in all, four loci (profound theological stance; realization or fulfillment; translation into temporal activity; wisdom for Christian ethics). With the advent of twentieth-century theology we can perhaps persuade ourselves that we know, better than past ages, something of the scope which a proper theological ethics ought to have. Most important, we have learned to recur to the idea of a theological beginning without giving up the other, tension-producing loci we have just illustrated. Karl Barth's view that Christian ethics is based upon the Word of God and is continuous with dogmatic reflection is the clearest and most convincing exposition of this rediscovery, especially as it appears in the first volume of his *Dogmatics*. But neither have we given up the great discovery of the nineteenth century, its conception of the substantiality of Christian ethics as a discipline which exists in some sense in its own right. Rather we have substituted the idea of the *interdependence* of ethics and dogmatics, trusting to insure that each discipline benefits from the other: ethics from the basis it receives out of theological insight, and dogmatics from the reminder it receives that God's word is a word received in living, willing, acting selves bound up with the conduct and misconduct of society at large. Helmut Thielicke, arguing for this interdependence of ethical and dogmatic thought, points to the shipwreck for ethics which a plan like Herrmann's invites if it is not modified. If the Christian faith is the source of moral strength but not of the idea of the good, then theology and religion must soon become secondary helping forces, instruments that afford some kind of spiritual power which enables us to do the good which they have not pointed us to, the good which perforce we must find somewhere else. In the final analysis man is "self-law" if not "self-power," and this can lead to the twentieth-century aberration: "Germany our goal, Christ our strength."[22]

In the thought of such twentieth-century ethicists as Reinhold Niebuhr, the importance accorded a theological stance has not shifted attention away from the other important loci of ethical fullness. Niebuhr insists upon relating ethical insights to worldly wisdom and upon viewing theological principles as action-complexes rather than as static things—as principles of transformation, as it were, which can change the conduct of men and societies, at least partially. His concern is best seen in his insistence that love is "approximated" in society in more or less ambiguous accessions of justice. To settle for an approximation of love is to make a far more modest claim for faith than to expect perfection with a Wesley. Also Niebuhr relates fulfillment to society rather than to the soul of the individual, and he raises the question of lack of historical fulfillment as a theological principle. But he does envisage approximations to *fulfillment* and so puts ethics to the test of adequacy in this respect.

We have already observed that Emil Brunner's *The Divine Imperative* is the best example of a twentieth-century theological ethics which sets a new standard for systematic completeness. If it is weakest at the very points (action and implementation) where Reinhold Niebuhr is strongest, then we can still point out that Brunner and Niebuhr together represent all of the major loci of Christian-ethical completeness. No previous century offered in its Christian-ethical disquisitions, in short, the range of loci which now occur to us.

So far we have noted the appearance, roughly in chronological order, of four main points of deliberate attention, or *loci*, of

Christian ethics, beginning with the introduction by Augustine of a governing theological stance (in his case, *caritas*) which wrought a reformulation of the conception of pious conduct in the ancient church.[23] Christian ethics here is bequeathed the formal category of a *theological underpinning for human conduct*. (And in fact the theological conception which for the most part has undergirded Protestant ethics was supplied at the Reformation, particularly in Luther's understanding of justification by faith as the basis of the Christian life.)

The next locus which comes to the point of deliberate attention is that of *fulfillment* (sanctification, or in some ways of thinking, perfection). This idea indeed is implicit in Augustine's ethics, for *caritas*, or the ability to love as theological criterion gives rise to the ethical notion of growth in grace which sanctifies conduct. In Protestantism the mainline Reformation stressed the theological stance of faith as a compendiously complete locus having its own ethical consequences. Thus the idea of fulfillment, never absent from the assumptions of Luther or Calvin, did not become a separate locus of ethical thinking. This is especially true of social and political fulfillment, though in most respects Calvin's thought was a little closer to our modern understanding of this problem than was Luther's. Most groups of the radical Reformation, on the other hand, tended to stress the *quality of the Christian life* as a more crucial phenomenon than the theological stance out of which that life flows. Perhaps the views of Menno Simons are the clearest example, although the later positions of the German pietists, Arminius, and the Wesleyans also illustrate the possibilities of this locus. (We have already pointed to Jonathan Edwards as a Protestant theologian who incorporated both loci, stance and fulfillment, as genuine elements in his ethical thinking.)

The third idea which becomes a deliberate sector of Christian-ethical thinking is the idea of temporal action or transformation, including the assumption that the movement from theological promise to ethical fulfillment involves a human response-action upon the plane of temporal society. There are two departures here from the orthodox Christian-ethical hope. First, the plane of realization becomes increasingly the world we live in. Second, the role of human beings, as selves and in groups, is steadily bolstered. In the most simplified form, this locus appears as the expectation of an earthly Kingdom of God. It appears in early form among Protestants, as Troeltsch and his successors point out, especially among some of the neo-Calvinistic sects. The Puritans, who are really neo-Reformed instead of neo-Calvinistic, and hardly a sect at all in America (unless we can call them an "established" sect), demonstrate the developments in their abortive efforts to lay out a holy commonwealth in New England, transforming the "wilderness" by their deeds and actions in response to the covenant offered them by God. Even clearer examples, to my mind, of the ingredients of "temporality" and "action" are the programs of the religious groups with incipient democratic ideals in seventeenth-century England, such as the Levellers and, as I have already observed, the ethical politics of the moderate theist, Thomas Jefferson. The Levellers seem to owe more to the Mennonites, a thoroughly separatist group on the Continent, than to Calvin, but their approach to the sins of the world is quite different from the world-denying solution of the Mennonites. Instead of retiring from society the Levellers inserted themselves boldly into the stream of English civil strife and proceeded to agitate for a number of civil liberties, such as the right to choose one's form of worship. Significantly, the Leveller procedure was to insist upon the political implementation of such biblical propositions as man's inherent dignity in virtue of his creation in the image of God.[24]

The fourth locus to become distinct was the nineteenth-century idea of the integrity or self-governance of ethics as a discipline of knowledge. I believe this locus is most helpfully to be considered now as a question about the distinctive insights which have to do with human conduct. These insights come on the one hand out of Christianity itself and the special media of knowledge through which revelational insight has traditionally been apprehended— Bible, tradition, conscience, theological reflection, and so on. On the other hand, these insights also come out of the ordinary media of human, secular, worldly wisdom as it bears upon human conduct. In other words, ethics for the Christian is dependent on theology, on one side, for it needs to know the basis upon which it stands, the distinctive promise held out for men in their lives when they live and act according to the point of view of their faith. But ethics is at the same time independent of theology in its co-equal dependence upon secular wisdom. Its task is a worldly one in that it must translate its theological stance into worldly action and must evoke authentic human conduct. For this side of its responsibility Christian ethics must call upon the whole range of worldly wisdom.

I propose then, in brief, four loci, or "common topics for ethical reflection" as the minimal points deserving attention in any reconstructed, twentieth-century Christian ethics. Given brief topical titles and rearranged logically rather than chronologically, we may refer to them as: *stance, wisdom, action,* and *fulfillment,* and we may specify their main formal content in the form of questions, each of which is to be answered in a separate part:

(1) What is the theological *stance,* the distinctive promise held out for man by the Judaeo-Christian faith, as a basis for his conduct, both personal and social?

(2) How are (a) the peculiar insights of this stance related to (b) the ordinary media of human, secular *wisdom,* and how may Christian ethics retain a proper interdependence with each?

(3) What are the appropriate modes of *action,* both personal and social, by which men may realize the promise vouchsafed in the stance?

(4) What criteria may be drawn upon to judge the actions of men and to test their realization of the promise? (In orthodox theology, this is the locus of sanctification; it is also related to the contemporary concern with eschatology; here it is called the locus of *fulfillment.*)

IV

HOW MUCH "COMPLETENESS"?

IT SHOULD BE CLEAR that these four loci do not function as an exhaustive statement of the contents of Christian ethics. Whatever vision of comprehensiveness we can put forward now will surely be questioned by the future, which will have, sooner or later, fuller notions of completeness for Christian ethics. More important, the twentieth century, as we have already noted, has been in some ways a century of breakdown for systematic theological and ethical thought. Christian ethics is especially vulnerable to the shock of the twentieth century, since much of the shattering of nineteenth-century values has turned upon social, ethical, and moral revolutions (e.g., in sexual morality, urbanization, race relations, the scale and standards of warfare). We can no longer necessarily rely upon such older ethical cements as natural law, the hegemony of the church, common moral consent, or that Protestant standby, the unilateral authority of the Bible. The impact of all this on Christian ethics is seen in the prominence in Protestantism of that school known as "contextual ethics." The contextualist prefers to base moral action upon ever-fresh readings of the "situation" and the continually renewed expectation of hearing God. Contextualism has a hold on at least part of the truth and there can be no further ethicizing in Protestantism that does not take into account the claims of the "situation" in shaping ethical answers. Yet contextualism taken obsessively leads only to the destruction of ethical thinking.

When I am asked by leaders of the more sophisticated Protestant denominational groups to speak to their college students I am usually proffered some form of the following forewarning: "They don't want easy answers or handed-down morality. They know there are no hard-and-fast rules any more. They know the

world has changed, and all they hope for are some new, fresh
ethical guidelines." That is to hope for a great deal. But the point
is well taken. We cannot, at least for now, expect to construct an
ambitious new system of Christian ethics. The world is still in
upheaval, and so is contemporary theology, for its part. Thorough
systematic work in Christian ethics must wait until the dust
settles—if it ever does. But the task of reflection is laid all the
same on those of us who live in the interregnum between Victorian morality and the coming "new" morality, between Barthian
theology and the coming "new" theology. The very fact of upheaval in moral and theological styles today argues for a renewed
attempt to think and rethink the problem of Christian ethics. We
cannot yet fill in the content of a systematic Christian ethics for
the last third of the twentieth century, but we can point, in the
style of a checklist, to certain loci or criteria[25] which will have to
be dealt with in any future Christian-ethical system. Given this
checklist, we can perhaps even say something about the directions and content of the loci themselves.[26]

NOTES

1. Erik H. Erikson, "Youth: Fidelity and Diversity," *Daedalus*, Winter
1962, p. 26.
2. We could retain the original identity of the terms "morality" and
"ethics" and then distinguish between the "conventional" and "critical"
approaches to morality or ethics. But this is cumbersome. On the other
hand, ethicists sometimes further refine the ethics-morality dichotomy into
a three-level schema. W. H. Werkmeister sees these three levels of investigation in ethics: (1) "the level of moral rules and imperatives as such, the
level of laws and commandments by which men actually or presumably
live . . . the level of morality proper." (2) " a . . . level of philosophical
inquiry . . . the level of ethical theories as such. The aim is here to
integrate moral codes much in the manner in which scientists integrate the
laws of nature, deriving them from certain initial definitions and postulates."
(3) ". . . a third level of philosophical inquiry at which we are concerned with the meaning of ethical statements and with the clarification of
. . . presuppositions . . . of ethical theories. This is the level of meta-
ethics. Here the ethical theories themselves are critically evaluated . . ."
W. H. Werkmeister, *Theories of Ethics: A Study in Moral Obligation*
(Lincoln, Neb.: Johnsen Publishing Co., 1961), pp. 409-10. I have com-
bined Werkmeister's second and third levels, ethical theory and its critical
evaluation into one level and have called it "ethics" in contrast with

"morality." Cf. Paul Tillich, *Morality and Beyond* (New York: Harper & Row, 1963), pp. 21-22.

3. Kenneth K. Bailey, *Southern White Protestantism in the Twentieth Century* (New York: Harper & Row, 1964), p. 145. In a study of religious groups in Detroit, Lenski found that "religious subcommunities *foster and encourage a provincial and authoritarian view of the world.*" In general the clergy were somewhat more free of this view, supporting, for example, a more liberal and humanitarian foreign policy, on the whole, than laymen. Gerhard Lenski, *The Religious Factor: A Sociological Study of Religion's Impact on Politics, Economics, and Family Life* (New York: Doubleday & Co., Anchor Books, 1963, rev. ed.), pp. 188, 314, 328.

4. New York *Times*, May 9, 1965; Nashville *Banner*, May 27, 1965.

5. Lenski, *op. cit.*, p. 317.

6. Karl Rahner, *Nature and Grace and Other Essays*, tr. Dinah Wharton (London: Sheed & Ward, 1963), p. 92.

7. Emil Brunner, *The Divine Imperative: A Study in Christian Ethics*, tr. Olive Wyon (London: Lutterworth Press, 1937).

8. For Barth's views, see especially his *Dogmatics*, Vol I/2, tr. G. T. Thomson and Harold Knight (New York: Charles Scribner's Sons, 1956), Section 23.3, "Dogmatics as Ethics," pp. 782-96. See also Vol. I/1, tr. G. T. Thomson (Edinburgh: T. & T. Clark, 1936), p. 132 and *passim* for expressions of his view of the primacy of God's word and deed over human formulations. Other "neo-orthodox" theologians whose ethical writings of one sort or another reflect these features include Rudolf Bultmann, Eduard Thurneysen, and Friedrich Gogarten. Reinhold Niebuhr's *The Nature and Destiny of Man* (New York: Charles Scribner's Sons, 1949), presents a mixture of these features with a thoroughly American sense of the applicability of theological motifs to society.

9. Thomas J. J. Altizer, "Nirvana and the Kingdom of God," in *New Theology No. 1*, ed. Martin E. Marty and Dean G. Peerman (New York: The Macmillan Co., 1964), pp. 151-53, 163.

10. Karl Barth, *The Epistle to the Romans*, tr. Edwyn C. Hoskyns from the sixth German ed. (London: Oxford University Press, 1933), pp. 50-51, 57, 74, and *passim*; Dietrich Bonhoeffer, *Letters and Papers from Prison* (London: SCM Press, 1953); Paul M. Van Buren, *The Secular Meaning of the Gospel* (New York: The Macmillan Co., 1963), pp. 137-48. See also Amos N. Wilder, "Christian Social Action and Existentialism," *Journal of Religion*, XL (July, 1960), 155-60. I have also benefited from Langdon Gilkey's unpublished paper, "Is God-Language Necessary?" an appraisal of the contrasts between neo-orthodoxy and the younger "God-is-dead" school.

11. William Hamilton, *"The New Essence of Christianity,"* (New York: Association Press, 1961), pp. 13, 14, 28, 119-20. While Hamilton belongs in the aforementioned "God-is-dead" school, it must be said that he hedges considerably here, and finally settles for the affirmation that God is merely absent for the nonce.

12. Gibson Winter, *The New Creation as Metropolis* (New York: The Macmillan Co., 1963), pp. 68-69.

13. Gabriel Marcel, in *Homo Viator: Introduction to a Metaphysic of Hope* (New York: Harper & Brothers, Harper Torchbooks, 1962) asserts that a stable order can be established on earth only "if man always remains acutely conscious that his condition is that of a traveller." Yet "we must begin by eliminating everything in any way connected with evolution from our

discussion. It has nothing to do with what we are considering here . . ." (p. 8). This insistence upon the existential as *opposed* to the temporal and physical strikes me as a new kind of world-denying pietism, and I find it to be a most common theme of both neo-orthodoxy and religious existentialism, visible in such diverse thinkers as Karl Barth, the early Bonhoeffer, Nicholas Berdyaev, and even Reinhold Niebuhr (see, for the latter, his view of original sin, in *The Nature and Destiny of Man*, I, Chs. 7-9, in which he labors to dissociate his thought from fundamentalism).

14. Paul Ramsey, *Basic Christian Ethics* (New York: Charles Scribner's Sons, 1950), xii; George F. Thomas, *Christian Ethics and Moral Philosophy* (New York: Charles Scribner's Sons, 1955); E. Clinton Gardner, *Biblical Faith and Social Ethics* (New York: Harper & Brothers, 1960). Gardner's book is openly indebted to the lectures of the late H. Richard Niebuhr, who would have published his own ethical system if he had lived; the beginnings of it are found in the posthumously published *The Responsible Self* (New York: Harper & Row, 1963).

15. I have chosen the venerable term "loci" deliberately as a formal designation of the several "places" or "points of focus" which ought to be singled out for deliberate study within the nexus of Christian-ethical thought. Philip Melanchthon's *Loci Communes* consists, he tells us, of an arrangement in methodical manner of "the most common topics of theological science." By the same token what I have in mind is a formal description of "the most common topics for ethical reflection." Melanchthon takes for the material content of the theological loci the principal doctrines—e.g., God, Trinity, Man, Faith, Sin, Law, Grace, and so on. I prefer to stress the formal character of the loci, i.e., the division of ethical study into procedural points of focus. But I do share Melanchthon's view that the theologian (or ethicist) ought to be responsible for gathering together the "principal topics" of his discipline, through which the whole of it might be comprehended, at least provisionally. I also agree with him that such effort ought not to be thought of as exhaustive. "I am indeed treating everything sparingly and briefly," he says, "I am only stating the nomenclature of the topics." In other words, the loci of Christian ethics are best to be regarded as a checklist, and a minimal one at that. *The Loci Communes of Philip Melanchthon*, tr. Charles Leander Hill (Boston: Meador Publishing Co., 1944), pp. 64-66.

16. See such writings of Augustine's as *De Opere Monachorum, De Bono Conjugali*, and *De Mendacio* or, even more to the point, the moral treatises of Tertullian. (St. Augustine's treatises are translated in *Nicene and Post-Nicene Fathers*, ed. Philip Schaff [Grand Rapids: Eerdmans Publishing Co., 1956] Vol. III as follows: "Of the Work of the Monks," pp. 503-24; "On the Good of Marriage," pp. 397-413; "On Lying," pp. 457-77.) As Helmut Thielicke puts it: "Where the theology of the ancient church takes up *ethical* problems, it either limits itself to practical casuistry, or else it remains, insofar as ethical principles are concerned, within the boundaries of dogmatics. In neither case is it interested in the independence of ethics, nor does this point really come up." (*Theologische Ethik*, I [Tübingen: J. C. B. Mohr, 1951, ¶¶ 82-84, 86.) But for an eloquent tribute to the importance of Augustine's introduction of a clear and profound theological principle as the basis of the Christian life, see Adolph Harnack, *History of Dogma* (New York: Russell and Russell, 1958), Vol. 5, pp. 61-94.

17. Ernst Troeltsch, *The Social Teaching of the Christian Churches*, tr.

Olive Wyon (New York: Harper & Brothers, Harper Torchbooks, 1960), II, 494-95. Thielicke's comment on the ethics of the Reformation is instructive. The Reformers' theology is full of ethical themes, novel, rich, and many-sided. Yet, all too often, Reformation ethics was lost in polemics, aimed at demonstrating either the potency of grace or the feebleness of works, or both. "The ethical remarks of Luther are in this sense nothing other than collected examples for the new evangelically disposed theology. This is by all means a great deal; but it is no founding of an 'ethics.'" Thielicke, *op. cit.*, I, ¶90. For a more positive appreciation of Luther as ethicist, see Karl Holl, *The Cultural Significance of the Reformation*, tr. Karl Hertz *et al.* (New York: Living Age Books, Meridian Books, 1959), p. 50 and *passim*. Luther comes closest to sustained ethical reflection, it seems to me, in such writings as "Temporal Authority: to What Extent It Should Be Obeyed," in *Luther's Works* (Philadelphia: Muhlenberg Press, 1962), Vol. 45, pp. 81-129; "Whether Soldiers, Too, Can Be Saved," and "On War Against the Turk," in *Works of Martin Luther* (Philadelphia: A. J. Holman Co., 1931), V, 34-74 and 81-123.

18. *The Life and Selected Writings of Thomas Jefferson*, ed. Adrienne Koch and William Peden (New York: Modern Library, 1944), pp. 277-79; Daniel J. Boorstin, *The Lost World of Thomas Jefferson* (Boston: Beacon Press, 1960), p. 194. Jefferson was not, as commonly supposed, a "deist," if by that we mean the advocate of a remote, passive God. Though he rejected the Trinitarian God and the Chalcedonian Christ of Christian orthodoxy, Jefferson held, unlike the classical deists, to a decidedly activist doctrine of God's work in the creation: "It is impossble, I say, for the human mind not to believe, that there is . . . an ultimate cause, a Fabricator of all things from matter and motion, their Preserver and Regulator while permitted to exist in their present forms, and their regeneration into new and other forms." (Letter to John Adams, 1823, p. 705 in *The Life and Selected Writings*) Jefferson's insistence upon the convertibility of theological principle into social and political reality is representatively seen in his First Inaugural Address, where he holds the nation to be "enlightened by a benign religion, professed, indeed, and practiced in various forms, yet all of them including honesty, truth, temperance, gratitude, and the love of man; acknowledging and adoring an overruling Providence, which by all its dispensations proves that *it delights in the happiness of man here and his greater happiness hereafter.* . . ." (*Ibid.*, p. 323, italics supplied). Government, Jefferson goes on to say, exists to provide a minimum framework of order and regulation to permit the realization of such blessings. To see how groups such as the Levellers and Diggers of the English Revolution were similarly informed by biblical understandings of human rights, see H. N. Brailsford, *The Levellers and the English Revolution* (London: Cresset Press, 1961), 78, 183-85, 659-62 and *passim*, and Christopher Hill, "The Norman Yoke," in *Puritanism and Revolution* (New York: Schocken Books, 1964), pp. 50-122.

19. W. Herrmann, *Ethik*, 5th ed. (Tübingen: J. C. B. Mohr, 1921), pp. 2, 10.

20. *Ibid.*, pp. 12, 17. Herrmann warns against referring the idea of moral self-direction to the single individual: "It is not correct that we can make our mission an inner freedom for ourselves alone. We become free only insofar as we succeed in placing ourselves in the service of an object,

the eternal right of which we are convinced about." *Ibid.*, p. 30. In what sounds like an anticipation in some respects of Bonhoeffer's "mature world" remarks, Herrmann points out that "only a morality which rests upon autonomous [*selbständiger*] knowledge" can truly serve the purposes of fellowship or know the confrontation with Jesus Christ as deliverance. In a polemical remark aimed at another remarkable theologian, Herrmann puts this idea succinctly: "Troeltsch cannot understand how one can move from the idea of autonomy to that of community, and that moral independence and submission to God belong together." (*Ibid.*, *Vorrede zur dritten Auflage*, xii.) See also Wilhelm Herrmann, *Faith and Morals*, tr. Donald Matheson and Robert Stewart (New York: G. P. Putnam's Sons, 1904), pp. 30, 121, 172.

21. It should be pointed out here that the view of "wisdom" which I develop in Part Three rejects Herrmann's view that moral truth is as independent of scientific or empirical knowledge as it is of dogma. I have tried to show that ethical wisdom is interdependent with both sacred and secular knowledge. See pp. 71–118 below.

22. Karl Barth, *Church Dogmatics*, I/2, *loc. cit.*; Roger L. Shinn, "Some Ethical Foundations of Christian Theology," *Union Seminary Quarterly Review*, XI (January, 1960), 99-110; Thielicke, *op. cit.*, I, ¶¶18, 19, 11. Thielicke sees this separation of ethical goal from Christian faith beginning with Melanchthon, continuing with Kant, and reaching classic expression with Herrmann.

23. Augustine's anti-Pelagian writings, according to Brunner, mark the point in Christian thought where Christian-ethical thinking based on principle begins (*The Divine Imperative*, p. 94).

24. Cf. Heinz Eduard Töcht, "Theologie der Gesellschaft oder Theologische Sozialethik?" *Zeitschrift für Evangelische Ethik*, IV (July, 1961), 217.

25. Here we follow Karl Barth, who replied as follows when a student asked him the difference between a "principle" and a "criterion": "A criterion is not a point of a programme. . . . All criteria are *approximations*. Principles are fixed. You cannot live by principles. . . . Criteria can only give directions." *Karl Barth's Table Talk*, ed. John D. Godsey (Richmond: John Knox Press, 1963), p. 82.

26. As we will show in more detail in Part Two, we do not intend to suggest the inviolability of the order of the loci or the necessary logical primacy of "stance." At this point, we raise only the issue of consistency: a truly systematic Christian ethics will envision means of action and tests of fulfillment, for example, which are in harmony with the character of the promise for man laid out in the stance.

Part Two

THE FIRST LOCUS:

STANCE

V

THE GROUND OF CHRISTIAN

ETHICS

ETHICS, AS WE DEFINE IT in Chapter I, consists in considered reflection about human actions from the point of view of some critical standard of excellence. But this definition leaves a great deal unsaid. Everything depends upon what our "critical standard of excellence" is, upon the way in which we see the purpose and quality of human activity. One familiar school of thought in philosophical ethics holds this critical standard to be well-being or happiness, and ethics thus consists of considered, critical reflection about the most appropriate human conduct for arriving at this state. Another takes obligation or duty to be this critical standard; human conduct is to be appraised ethically according to the degree that it manifests willing performance of duty. The alternatives are many and varied, and our first task is to gain some definiteness in our conception of what the Christian alternative(s) may be.

Nearly all Christian ethicists employ, either openly or implicitly, some kind of critical standard of excellence, ordinarily drawn from one or more of the distinctive teachings of the Christian faith. What is more, the perceptive ethicist is very much aware that he proceeds from some particular "stance." Christian ethics, according to H. Richard Niebuhr, begins not by asking first, "What shall we do?" but turns instead to the prior question of the impact upon human conduct wrought by the "presence of Jesus Christ in . . . our history." Before there can be a "Christian social ethic," Paul Ramsey argues, "understanding of the fundamental moral perspective of the Christian must be deepened and clarified." Even an avowed contextualist who thinks we must get our bearings in the changing actual situation is still aware, as a careful thinker, of the role played by the input of a stance: "As a theological discipline," Paul Lehmann says, "ethics involves reflection upon life, upon the cement of human society, and upon morality from the standpoint of certain theological presuppositions."[1]

All of these statements point in the same direction: Christian ethics must contend as a primary challenge with the question of its theological ground and competence, *its origin in some expectation for the life and conduct of man under God distinctive in the Judaeo-Christian tradition.* It is the task of the systematic Christian ethicist, soon or late, to ferret out this expectation, to specify as a theological benchmark just what kind of critical standard of excellence the Christian faith furnishes for men. This is why the Christian ethicist can never proceed in an entirely autonomous fashion, for he is always in need of the specialized talents of biblical interpreters, church historians, and systematic theologians to help him understand, for his own time and place, the distinctively Christian conception of what it means to live and act as a human being. (He himself, of course, may be more or less competent in one or more of these disciplines.) Only by rethinking, with the technical assistance of these several branches of theological learning, the meaning of the Christian faith for human conduct, can he ever hope to offer an appropriate and helpful, i.e., saving, ethics to men of his own time.

Protestantism normally has taken for its critical standard of excellence in human conduct (or, we may say more compendiously, for its stance) the theological reality of *faith.* Trust and confidence in Jesus Christ are all that is demanded to win the favor of God, which favor in turn is the basis of salvation, or redemption from frailty and sin. Right conduct flows out of faith. "The good consists simply and solely in the fact that man receives and deliberately accepts his life as a gift from God," says Emil Brunner, "as life dependent on 'grace,' as the state of 'being justified' because it has been granted as a gift as 'justification by faith.'" Among the more imaginative recent modifications of this stance in Protestantism we might mention the approach of Paul

Lehmann, who proposes that "life in the *koinonia*" or Christian fellowship be the ground of ethics. The starting point for Christian-ethical thinking, he tells us, "is the fact and the nature of the Christian church." In the *koinonia* "it makes sense to talk about the will of God as the answer to the question: What am I, as a believer in Jesus Christ and as a member of his church, to do?"[2]

As another example of a contemporary Protestant reformulation of orthodox Protestantism on the stance we may point to the developing ethics of Paul Ramsey, who has used the symbols "Exodus" and "Egypt" to denote the idea that Christian ethics does not begin or proceed apart from notions of natural law, but that the latter are always being overcome, revised, and transformed by the appearance among men of *agape*. In short, the route to the Christian expectation is one of an "Exodus" from the "Egypt" of natural law. "In-principled love" is another key concept of Ramsey's to indicate that *agape* comes into the forms and orders of the natural world ("principles" in this case) in order to work its transformations. Ramsey's stance is more than a revision of the distinctive Protestant insistence upon the primacy of faith. Like the earlier ethics of Jonathan Edwards, it holds forth a vision of the natural order which grace, through faith, is to transform. Augustine, Edwards, and Ramsey think more directly of *love*, moreover, as the criterion of human conduct, than do Luther, Calvin, and Brunner, who employ *faith* more consistently as the basic expression of the Christian stance for ethics.[3]

To take one more example of a contemporary Protestant reformulation of the stance for ethics, H. Richard Niebuhr in his posthumously published *The Responsible Self* begins by comparing the Christian faith with two leading alternatives in philosophical ethics. On the one hand, there is the old view, still followed, which thinks of man as "maker," interested in purposive action, the realization of an end (classical teleology and eudaemonism, the ethic of "happiness"). On the other hand there is the picture of man as "citizen," which holds that the impulse to duty, or consent to law, is true virtue (seen classically in Kant). Niebuhr believes that the Christian faith evokes a third picture of ethical man, and this is man who sees his conduct historically in terms of persistent dialogue, query and response, action according to what one decides to be "fitting" in the situation before God and neighbor. One's goal is reconciliation but he has to find out how to reach it, and indeed in a sense, what it is, by communication. "At the critical junctures in the history of Israel and of the early Christian community," says Niebuhr, "the decisive question men raised was not 'What is the goal' nor yet 'What is the law' but 'What is happening?' and then 'What is the fitting response to what is happening?'" That which is happening to man is most profoundly understood as the presence and impact of Jesus Christ in human history. This presence sets in motion a "cause," which becomes the highest criterion of human actions. This cause is "bringing God to men and men to God and so also of reconciling men to each other and to their world." From this stance of reconciliation—known only as it emerges in human dialogue—Niebuhr argues the distinctiveness of Christian ethics as consisting of responsive, fitting action aimed at reconciliation.[4]

This is not the place to argue which stance is most appropriate for Christian ethics today. Our point is to observe that every comprehensive statement of Christian ethics builds upon a stance and that the task of clarifying this stance and making it relevant to the life and deeds of his fellows at his own time and in his own place is always laid upon the reflective Christian ethicist. In the following chapter we will investigate some of the problems attending the traditional Protestant stance of "faith," and in the final chapter of this part, we will suggest a new stance characterized as "promise and fulfillment." In the meantime let us round out our formal description of the category of the stance with these corollaries:

1. Stance as originally ethical.

We are not to infer because the stance is to be described by theological inquiry that this means it is not really or yet a part of "ethics." We are not to conclude that we learn what our stance is from the systematic theologian or dogmatician and then as ethicists take it and apply it further along the line, now making something ethical or practical out of it. This would be to misunderstand the fully ethical orientation of Protestant theology itself. To take the conventional Protestant stance of faith, for example, we can be sure that faith at the very outset is already a laying hold of the promise from God of a *new life* or *freshly consecrated actions,* so it is not only a theological notion, but an ethical one as well. Indeed, there is a sense in which the ethicist is dependent upon the systematic theologian, just as he is dependent on the specialist in Old Testament or patristics, to give him information and insight which he then uses in his own right as a thinker. But it is also true that the systematic theologian is dependent upon the ethicist. "In order to understand the Christian faith and spiritual events [*Vorgänge*]," W. Herrmann insists, and here we agree, "one must proceed from a comprehension of morality."[5] If we interpret this thought in a manner somewhat less zealous for the total autonomy of ethics than Herrmann's, we can say its meaning to us is this: in order to understand the Christian faith itself, one must be ready to translate it into the lexicon of human response-activity, i.e., into the terms of Christian ethics. The purpose of God's work among men, according to classical Protestantism, is to draw them to him and evoke their praise. But this is continuous with the thought that the purpose of his work is to renew man and to deliver him into a new humanity, so he may praise God aright. "It would be false," Thielicke comments, "to understand ethics as a discipline in which the 'practical consequences' of faith are drawn, and which would be added to the theoretical undertaking of Dogmatics as a practical epilogue." Faith must be regarded as the content of both dogmatics and ethics, even though at the point of laying out a stance, we must call upon the special theological tools of investigation.[6]

2. Stance as logically prior.

By placing the question of a stance first, we do make a provisional judgment as to its relative importance and priority. But we do not thereby fix universally the sequence of steps in ethicizing.

As we have already noted,[7] the ethical thought of Reinhold Niebuhr begins, if at any one locus, at the point of "temporal action"
(our third locus), as does the vital enterprise of the Social Gospel
which preceded him. Niebuhr started off by working at the problem of rectifying injustices done the working man rather than of
reciting the doctrines of God, man, and salvation which might
give theoretical orientation to such a project. His earlier writings
dwell predominantly upon this locus of temporal action. Only in
his mature period as teacher of Christian ethics does his approach
substantially involve digging underneath to lay bare the theological presuppositions of social action. Two treatises of this mature
period, *An Interpretation of Christian Ethics* and *The Nature and
Destiny of Man,* constitute in effect this secondary movement to
clarification of the theological stance. It must be recorded, however, that the analogous movement from the locus of action to the
locus of stance in the career of Niebuhr's forerunner, Walter
Rauschenbusch, did not have so happy an outcome. Rauschenbusch, too, is first conscious of the challenge of Christian ethics
primarily at the point of temporal action, and only as an anti-
climax to his career does he ask reflectively for the stance in his *A
Theology for the Social Gospel.* While this book is impressive in a
sense and has enjoyed a certain revival upon seminary reading
lists, it is really used today only as a compendious historical ex-
hibit, and not as a piece of theological inquiry. It lacks the profundity of Niebuhr's theological retractations and did not have
the effect of correcting and critically modifying social ethics as
Niebuhr's considered work has done. On the other hand, Rauschenbusch's earlier books, written more as descriptions of the
task of social action, are convincing documents.[8]

In general it should be clear that our arrangement of the loci,
with stance placed first, does not foreshadow a consideration of
the remaining loci as dependent rungs of a ladder. We propose
the loci rather as a checklist of dimensions proper to minimal
comprehensiveness in Christian-ethical inquiry. At the same time,
this is not to say that there is no inner relation among the loci in a
systematic discussion of Christian ethics. It will become clearer as
we discuss the other three loci that we view them collectively as

belonging to each other as much as, say, the four quadrants of a circle's arc belong to the whole circle. Still, the circle does not "begin" necessarily at any one of the quadrants. The precise relation between any two of the loci is a function of the content of the ethical system.

3. Stance as source of criteria.

The task of the theological ethicist is always to present the *distinctive* elements of a critical standard of excellence which is to be found in the Christian faith (or, more broadly, the Judaeo-Christian tradition). "Distinctive" as used here is a dual concept. It refers first and most importantly to the vision or expectation for human conduct that is *permanently* peculiar to the Judaeo-Christian tradition. It refers in the second place to the special insights out of this reservoir which this tradition may deliver anew *in changed times*, or after an epochal crisis, when the Gospel—the promise and reality of wholeness for man—must be retranslated for a new generation, and particular strands of this tradition, not so relevant before, suddenly become of burning importance. Thus I believe that the biblical tradition has permanent implications for human wholeness that are distinctive to it alone, but that certain of them are particularly distinctive for the twentieth century, with its racial struggles, in a way not realized, or needed to be realized, before. Yet to search out and present what is "distinctive" does not mean to rely exclusively upon the sacred media of revelation. There is a complex and inescapable relation between the media of revelation and secular wisdom. This relation was oversimplified as one of *continuity* by freewheeling liberal theologians of the late nineteenth century, who saw God in everything from test tubes to the YMCA. It was oversimplified as one of *discontinuity* in the early classical documents of neo-orthodoxy, e.g., the writings of the younger Karl Barth. We shall have to treat the relation between these sources, revelation and worldly wisdom, as a dialectical one involving both continuity and discontinuity.

4. Stance as servant of Gospel.

It is the task of the Christian ethicist to think out the implications of the Judaeo-Christian faith for human conduct and to formulate a stance that registers what is distinctive from this source. Yet we must recognize that no given stance will actually be adequate to the whole Gospel. The Gospel is the promise and reality itself of new life; the theologian's stance is an expression of this promise and reality. Whereas every stance we set forth partakes of some rational, even ideological, position relative to the challenges that confront us, the Gospel itself is non-ideological and universal in its healing powers. The Gospel may speak for a given time and purpose through a certain stance, and through one stance more effectively than another. But it is not to be identified fully and finally with any of them. It is especially not to be permanently identified with religious ideologies or partial theological affirmations. In this sense, the traditional Catholic criticism of Luther's overemphasis upon "faith alone" and belief in right doctrine is now becoming more relevant. If Catholics are beginning to revise aspects of their own stance today, they also properly insist that Luther took some "perfectly Catholic principles" and "asserted them with a one-sided stress" (Hans Küng). Every stance, we must say, however workable and true to biblical scholarship it may appear to be in its time, must be taken as provisional, subject to restatement under the impact of the total Gospel and of new times. But this is only another way of underlining the urgency of new reflection toward a fresh stance for Christian ethics that will serve the last part of the twentieth century. The older stances, in particular the orthodox formulas of justification by faith, tend to become ideologies now, no longer communicating the power and relevance of the Gospel itself for the life and deeds of men.[9]

school of younger theologians who suspect that God is either dead or missing, and who boldly question that favorite doctrine of neo-orthodoxy, God's otherness or transcendence.[11] This movement, even if it is mistaken, may do us the service of jarring those advocates of Christian ethics who have been insisting that "the new theology" has the answers to moralism, on the one side, and secularism, on the other. On second inspection, much of "contextualist" Christian ethics is actually a quest for ways of incarnating this already taken-for-granted theological position into the situation rather than, as the name "contextualist" implies, any genuine openness toward learning to change our minds.

Nowhere, I believe, has this fixation upon a possibly irrelevant theological stance been so marked as among the proponents of justification by faith as the theological underpinning for American social ethics. Part of the difficulty with the formation of social ethics in America since the late 1920's has been the uncritical adulation with which admittedly important European thinkers are received. A prime case in point is the regard for Dietrich Bonhoeffer, the penetrating theological ethicist whose career was cut off at the end of World War II by the fleeing Nazis who held him prisoner. I am not thinking so much of the current veneration paid him by the theologians of secular salvation as of the cult of demipietists and part-time existentialists which gathered about him a few years ago. This following, which manifested strong interests in ecumenicity and renewal of the church, was not electrified so much by Bonhoeffer's late apology for secular revelation, *Letters and Papers from Prison,* as by his earlier crypto-pietist writings, *The Cost of Discipleship* and *Life Together.* Several memorable phrases from Bonhoeffer served only to reinforce among American Christians a dubious misuse of the Protestant stance that has been abroad in Protestantism since the Reformation. One of these is Bonhoeffer's epithet, "cheap grace."[12] Bonhoeffer uses it rightly to chastise those Christians who abuse Luther's understanding of faith and assume that by the mere act of "belief" they are saved enough, and relieved of the responsibility of "works"—of hard, tedious ethical witness to the Word of God. This is to miss the whole point of the watchword, *sola fide.* It is "cheap grace," Bonhoeffer insists, to think one can have God's favor purely through assent to right doctrine, while he bears no burdens, pays no price, makes no sacrifices. Luther had indeed spoken of the initiative of God and the character of grace as a free gift, not buyable by good works. But to take Luther as saying the saved are dispensed from ethical witness is to subscribe to lazy, fraudulent Christianity.

Surely Bonhoeffer is right. Religion is sorely abused in America, too, by lazy, passive, unconcerned Christians. And yet, I submit, the temptation to cheap grace is *not* the principal heresy of American Christianity and never has been. The trouble with the Puritan-spawned, frontier-hardened American psyche is not any yearning to take our blessings casually. The problem with American Christianity, indeed, with American life itself, is of a quite opposite character. It is the temptation to make grace too *costly*, to insist that we "merit" it, to strive to save ourselves by backbreaking good works. Thus the good church member and businessman who seems oblivious to the ethical demands laid upon him, say, by the civil rights movement is probably not best described as a devotee of cheap grace. On the contrary, he is likely to think of himself as having "proved himself" by hard work, and to take the point of view that the disinherited and poverty-stricken must win through to blessedness by the same route.

The conditional covenant of the Puritans, which provided a place for good works as a sign of divine election, was only a mild, respectable form of what became on the frontier an out-and-out activism. "Religion is something to do," insists the noted nineteenth-century revivalist, Charles Grandison Finney, "not something to wait for." Americans are determined to work for the grace they receive, even if it kills them, and kills God, too (the latter by the very implication that grace is not a gift).[13]

It is true that many of the mainline American denominations have always left a place, theoretically, for the primacy of justification by faith: Congregationalists, Presbyterians, Baptists, and Methodists have advocated it heartily—on paper. But the genius of none of these groups in the American experience is to be explained by any theological concept approximating Luther or

Calvin's understanding of *sola fide;* they have all stressed the primacy of the Christian life rather than of saving beliefs, at least where ethical witness is concerned. We could consider the great religiously inspired or church-supported reform movements in this country, for example: extension of the franchise, abolition, temperance, the Social Gospel, moral criticism of political corruption, racial integration. In each of these reforms, theological motifs other than justification by faith were operative. Perhaps more than any other, the doctrine of creation was influential, with its high place for man and the intimation of equality found in the *imago dei* teaching (Genesis 1:26-31, Psalms 8). Justification by faith has usually been accompanied by a more or less narrow doctrine of election which, when translated into political terms, entails "the assumption that the Elect (those chosen by God or through the agency of His Grace for salvation) should rule over the rest of mankind."[14] On the other hand, the Protestant conception of the equality of all men—or at least the equality of all believers capable of reading Scripture for themselves—decisively nourished the modern ideas of political and civil equality.

Protestant social ethics in America all along has been based on justification by faith only in a nominal sense. In operation, different theological underpinnings have been far more central: the conditional covenant in New England, with its expectation that God would limit himself in recognition of his human partners; the exuberant confidence in man's inventiveness and sense of injustice among the American rationalists and politically oriented Christians (Thomas Jefferson and Abraham Lincoln, to name two); the strong insistence that grace is mediated through dexterous human activity, often running to improvisation, which characterized frontier religion.[15]

Only Jonathan Edwards, of the great American theologians through the middle of the nineteenth century, found an ethical stance both appropriate to the American ethos and zealous of the proper concerns of the justification-by-faith motif. Edwards forges ahead of the Reformation by constructing a whole criteriology of the states of the self as a way of viewing the impact of grace. Above all, Edward sees that every doctrine of God implies a doctrine of man and that henceforth the theologian cannot speak of divine activity by contrasting it with human inactivity:[16]

> In efficacious grace we are not merely passive, nor yet does God do *some*, and we do the *rest*. But God does all, and we do all. God produces all, and we act all. For that is what he produces, viz. our own acts. God is the only proper author and fountain: *we only are the proper actors.*

We shall have to return to this view of Edwards', for it points us in the right direction. But first, however, we must say more about the Reformation formula *sola fide*. To demonstrate that it has never really functioned as stance for much of American Christianity is by no means to furnish grounds for restating it in different terms. Rather, we must attempt any such restatement only because we are driven to it by the inability of the older formula to point to the salvation of man in our time.

The sixteenth-century view of justification by faith, I believe, is tied to an anthropology unable to account for the exploding initiative of secular ("natural") man since the eighteenth century. In aim the formula *sola fide* has perennial truth and strength. Luther and Calvin meant to insure that men discern the source of their wholeness in the forgiveness and love of God. They affirmed blessedness as a reality that begins in God, and faith as a recognition of this state of affairs. They spoke of faith *alone* to guard against destructive *hubris* and self-centeredness. Nevertheless, the Reformation formula, if it is to guide us now, must be demythologized on two counts.

1. To say *sola fide* is to invoke an obsolete view of human capacity which implies that natural man is "altogether passive" until he has been "quickened and renewed by the Holy Spirit" (*Westminster Confession*, X, 2).

The knowledge of both God and self, says Calvin, "principally consists in renouncing all idea of our own strength, and divesting ourselves of all confidence in our own righteousness." Our moral powers are not only unequal to the task of representing God's will, they are "altogether null." Human capacity in itself, far from testifying to an origin in God, only shows how unworthy man is of claiming this origin. "We cannot be permitted to measure the glory of God by our ability." Faith, then, is proposed as an act of rescue and a sharp alternative to human impotency. "Feeling his utter inability to pay what he owes to the Law, and thus despairing of himself," man confronted by God "bethinks him of applying and looking to some other quarter for help" (*Institutes*, II. viii. 1-3).[17]

The twentieth century's problem with this way of putting it is that no place is left for the significance of natural or secular human activity and initiative. Indeed, the tendency here is to stress, for secular man, *passivity* as a posture more amenable to God's purposes than initiative and activity. I do not overlook the humanism of Calvin's thought, or the humanness of Luther's, or the activity and initiative that both saw as characterizing men of faith. It was Luther, after all, who called faith a "busy, living, active thing" and insisted upon the response to Christ of taking the lead, serving as Christ to one's neighbor. Calvin and his followers were vigorous activists and Reformed theology bred one of the most furious movements of "doers" of all, the Puritans. Both, in short, understood faith to consist of two aspects: (1) a state of receptivity to that which is offered in the divine grace (a state best thought of as "trust"); (2) a state of grateful and active response, empowered by the divine grace (a state best thought of as "witness" or "service"). Yet all this sense of initiative and activity, I fear, was firmly connected to the empowerment of redeeming grace, and natural or secular man, lacking this rehabilitating aid, is invariably pictured as impotent, strengthless, and passive. Insisting stoutly on the possibility of action on the part of redeemed man, yet the Reformers fell back upon a conception of unredeemed man that equated natural activity with futility, illusion, and sin. By implication the only valid role left to secular man is the passive openness to hearing of his own lostness. This office of natural man is summed up in the Reformation's view of the "religious" function of the Law, which acts as a hammer (Luther) or mirror (Calvin), bringing the sinner to his knees in despair and reducing his unredeemed acts to the status of worthlessness. Even Karl Holl, whose researches demonstrate the cultural and ethical richness of the Reformation, is clear that the "joy in activity" that Luther and Calvin commend is not inherent in natural man, but only "in the nature of the man reborn in God." Indeed, for Luther, the "old Adam" is a loafer; it is only the true Christian who works with zest and zeal.[18]

This low estimate of natural activity persisted in Protestant thought and found gifted expression in the very place we might least expect it: liberalism. Despite Schleiermacher's departures from the Reformers on other fronts, he continues to affirm that religion is not a doing or activity, but rather an inward state that he describes as a feeling of absolute dependence. "To feel oneself absolutely dependent and to be conscious of being in relation with God are one and the same thing." We are not surprised, then, when Schleiermacher, considering the two-sidedness of faith (receptivity and active response) concludes that "the element of receptivity, in some way or other affected, is the primary one."[19]

The most eloquent apologist for the passive view of man in our time is not Karl Barth, but a troubled young woman who died a near-Catholic, Simone Weil. Man's movement to salvation is for her essentially a kind of "looking or listening." Obedience is a "passive" thing, as far as possible from "muscular effort." There is only waiting, silence, immobility. "The attitude which brings about salvation is not like any form of activity. . . . The slave, who waits near the door so as to open immediately the master knocks, is the best image of it."[20]

However forthrightly we must still insist on the efficacy of God's grace, in the twentieth century we can no longer make the point by drawing a contrast with natural actions—as our fascination with secular man "come of age" clearly attests. It may be, indeed, that the chief problem of contemporary theology is not that God is dead, but that man is alive. It may be that even today we have not come resolutely to grips with the doctrine of man: his natural, unredeemed, secular initiative as a sign of his origin in the divine creation. Whether we realize it or not, says Karl Rahner, "whatever is healthy or morally fine or well ordered and harmonious, even apparently on the purely human level, is . . . a manifestation of grace and the divine life." When these things heal man, "it does not make this salvation any the less God's action that it also comes about, and must do, through our action, for our action is already his grace."[21]

Natural human activity, in short, must now be assigned a primary place rather than an ancillary one in theological investigation. God speaks through human acts and words as well as through receptivity and silence, for either state is at best a kind of finite witness to the divine. I would argue that on the whole the divine initiative and grace are now more faithfully mediated through the symbols of human initiative (especially at the level of human relations, but not excluding "muscular effort") than otherwise. We will always need the complementary symbols of receptivity, to be sure, for silence, emptiness, and dependence will continue to symbolize one aspect of man's stance before God. But in any case one must represent divinity with the materials of his own culture, and since the Enlightenment, Western man's inevitable discovery of himself has rendered inaccurate the older view of man as in and of himself ethically and socially incompetent.

Nietzsche and the existentialists caught the new idea in their common insistence that Christianity cannot be taken henceforth as a belief so much as a mode of existence. One finds selfhood and reality in his actions: that is the basis of humanity and virtue. We live in what Edward T. Hall calls an "ageric" culture (from Latin *agere*, to act), denoting a culture that makes a distinction between activity and dormancy and insists on doing things as a way of conceiving time. This mode of seeing reality is most characteristic of North America and Northern Europe. In certain other cultures, including the Navajo and many of those of the East, no distinction is made between being active and being passive. Hence time passes in any case, and it makes no difference whether one does something or not. But Americans and other ageric moderns are different. "With us we have to work to get ahead. We do not get ahead automatically."[22]

The question is not whether the ageric outlook is proper or improper, for it is ingrained and operative. The question is whether man shall use his activeness and self-reliance to serve himself or serve God and the neighbors. Whatever we may conclude, we must begin with the view that man is an active, self-reliant creature, created that way: that is his *imago dei*.

2. To say *sola fide* is to introduce an unintended theological cleavage between faith and culture and to obscure the cultural and social significance of the Reformation itself.

Not only the researches of Karl Holl, but the studies of such contemporary American Christian ethicists as H. Richard Niebuhr and Paul Lehmann have shown the positive contribution of the Reformers toward enriching, as Holl puts it, "all areas of culture." One thinks of Luther's insistence that believers should be able to read the Bible for themselves, and thus be literate; or Calvin's understanding of the Church as the transformer of worldly society into the "Holy community."

It is because I accept this appreciative estimate of the Reformation that I venture to quarrel with the watchword, *sola fide,* and the theological claims that accompany it, especially in the thought of Luther. In discussing the meaning of faith, Luther deliberately introduces a tension into the Christian life. Faith leads to inward peace with God and eternal blessedness, but it does not offer hope of temporal betterment. In his own theology Luther fixes temporal welfare in the realm of the Law rather than in that of the Gospel. He was dismayed and angered when the peasants acted against their temporal lords in the name of the Gospel, seeking to improve their earthly situation. They had misunderstood the Gospel and his own teaching of Christian liberty, he bitterly complained. Justification by faith for Luther, in other words, carries with it in theory a qualitative distinction between time and eternity, between world and Kingdom of God, and the fruits of faith are not to be expected in the form of temporal, worldly benefits.[23]

Contemporary Protestant social ethics claims at one and the same time to build upon the Reformation idea of faith, and yet to regard the secular, temporal life as a genuine locus of the Gospel. We continue to sound the Reformation slogans, whilst in practice we have departed from the old stance, taking temporality to be the representative and bearer of eternity, and seeing the possibilities of faring well in the temporal realm as an approximation, at least, of Gospel wholeness. This newer understanding is embodied, for example, in the Niebuhrian axiom, widely and cheerfully sworn by in American neo-orthodoxy, that social justice is an implementation or fragmentary step toward the impossible fullness of love.

The contributions of Luther and the other Reformers to democracy, literacy, and a joyful affirmation of life and work is vast, and as I have already said, my point is not to argue otherwise. But I do contend that the formula *sola fide* and its corollary in Luther's mind, the doctrine of the two realms, deny in theory the very same cultural, social, and political benefits of grace we are anxious to proclaim. Luther's doctrines should not be regarded as deliberately anti-social but only as ineffectual to express the societal implications of the Gospel. Luther indeed sets the stage for the modern emergence of man as displayer of initiative, and this preparation is focused, moreover, in Luther's view of faith. With Luther, the Christian now believes in his own right and person (by way of Scripture) and does not depend for his substance on a priestly hierarchy. But the *forms* in which Luther and the other Reformers stated these revolutionary ideas—*sola fide, sola scriptura,* the two realms, and so on—depend on a theoretical cleavage between faith and culture that is no longer necessary, or tolerable. To the extent that the doctrine of justification by faith points the believer to a realm of "Gospel" that contrasts with the hard, temporal, commercial, legal, fleshly realm of "Law," it sets him apart, without exactly intending to, from his true surroundings. It isolates the victim of society from a portion of his salvation, the temporal benefits that he needs; it conceals from those better off their responsibilities to temporal society.[24]

Thoughtful Protestants, then, will agree with the Catholic historian Christopher Dawson that, whatever the merits of the Reformation, one problem was its tendency in doctrinal statements to drive a wedge between faith and cultural phenomena. Dawson is overly critical when he minimizes the fundamental contribution of Protestantism to literacy and education. Yet there is more than a grain of truth in his contention that Christianity and culture are far more interdependent than the salvation teachings of the Reformation allowed for. The cleavage continued and in some ways worsened among the inheritors of the Reformation. John Wesley resolved to be a "man of one book"—*homo unius libri;* fortunately, R. Newton Flew observes, he never kept his promise. But his Methodist followers all too literally did keep it. John Pawson burned Wesley's Shakespeare with its copious notes from Wesley's hand. "The result of this inward asceticism was a sharp division of life into sacred and secular."[25]

Not all of this cleavage must be laid to the defects of the justification by faith doctrine. Among Methodists and Baptists the sectarian, world-denying tendency was also noticeable. Yet in American Christianity we see this schism maintained, more often than not, in the name of "faith alone." Whereas a certain realization that the church is in but not of the world would be beneficial, American churchmen have too often stressed instead the isolation of religion from politics, scientific knowledge, and social concern. We see the cleavage in the intellectual and theological shallowness that runs through Protestant theological education. The putative sufficiency of faith alone, and its analogue, *sola scriptura,* constitute the standard pretext.

This cleavage between faith and culture is only intensified by the two-valued view of good and evil that is bound up with the *sola fide* teaching. According to orthodox Protestantism, man is either lost or blessed, and there is no gradation, no halfway point in between. Man in his natural state and, by implication, the nations, his society, and his culture are lost. "The Word of God leaves no half life to man," says Calvin, "but teaches that in regard to life and happiness, he has utterly perished" (*Institutes,* II. v. 19). Commenting on Calvin's 1542 Catechism, Karl Barth sounds this note again in our own day:[26]

> The choice which man has can only be that between "the highest good" and the "greatest misery." There is no intermediate stage between a fulfilled and a wasted human life. Hence there are no lesser goods in the attainment of which man could still be human even though he missed this highest good.

On the contrary, human culture is palpably an imposing mosaic of goods and values, finite and discolored with human frailty, to be sure, but potent in diverse ways to reflect and express what is human, for all that. Those who live in it, irrespective of their religious faith, represent an immense spectrum of degrees of fulfillment. Hence the formula *sola fide,* if taken rigorously, requires twentieth-century man to shut his eyes to the formidable array of partial, but helping, goods which manifests itself in the secular or natural side of every society. In this respect, the more mellow, moderate Catholic appraisal of man and culture, which understands "natural" man as capable of limited, though not of saving, fulfillment, is simply truer to the realities of the urban twentieth century.

I have gone to some length to express my qualms about the formula *sola fide* and the anthropology that goes with it. The reason is not only that the formula in orthodox style has in recent years enjoyed a revival, but also that it has reappeared in American neo-orthodoxy in a sophisticated, disguised form and as such has become the most prevalent stance in American Protestant theology for appraising society and culture. I refer to the point of view—stemming from Paul Tillich, old-fashioned existentialists, and a certain agrarian outlook allergic to technology—that the predicament of man in modern industrial society is best described as one of "meaninglessness." Viktor E. Frankl puts this mood well (though it is not his own position). In our day man is threatened "by his existential vacuum, by his 'living' nihilism." Scores consider their lives meaningless, "see no meaning in their personal existence and therefore think it valueless."[27] The resemblance of this modern estimate of man to the estimate of culture implied in the Reformation formula *sola fide* is apparent. Though it has been espoused by unbelievers as far apart as H. L. Mencken and Albert Camus, it is, I believe, largely a contemporary reconstruction in semantic terms of some motifs of the older formula.

The link to the Reformation is expressly clear in the thought of Tillich, who consciously relates today's question of meaninglessness to the older Protestant answer of justification by faith. Paul's question, "How do I become liberated from the law?" and Luther's question, "How do I find a merciful God?" are replaced in our period by the question, "How do I find meaning in a meaningless world?" For Luther natural man was incapable of doing good works. For Tillich, on the other hand, natural man is certainly potentially capable of finding meaning; yet our present situation, he says, is characterized by "a profound and desperate feeling of meaninglessness," applicable both to individuals and groups.[28]

Despite the contemporaneity of his theology, in his appraisal of the human situation Tillich now and then almost seems to recur to the cultural anthropology of the sixteenth century. To be sure, for him the development of wholeness in men is a process realized in life, in which persons become increasingly self-aware, free, related to others, and open to the transcendent. Tillich properly insists upon the partial character of all that is realized naturally, short of the healing advent of the "New Being." Human relations alone "cannot conquer loneliness, self-seclusion, and hostility. . . . Relatedness needs the vertical dimension in order to actualize itself in the horizontal dimension." And yet this mode of depicting man's plight and his hope of salvation surely re-echoes the old cleavage between intervening grace (if not deity in Tillich's case) and helpless creature, for faith is identified as promising only by contrast with a despairing, meaningless-prone culture. (There is even a doctrine of election, a kind of corporation of the saved entailed here, namely, the professional classes, the upper bourgeois, the sophisticated—those for whom religion is a question of meaning and the handling of semantic symbols, of relating, of self-conscious deliberation and decision making. It is these who with the help of the "vertical" are able to find meaning and thus salvation.)[29]

Doubtless the diagnosis that life is meaningless does describe the affliction of millions of bourgeois and intellectual Europeans in the aftermath of World Wars I and II. Undoubtedly it describes the outlook of many Americans. H. L. Mencken not only called human existence "essentially meaningless," but likened it to "a disease of the cosmos." But Mencken was a writer and editor, and in this sense a type of intellectual. We may seriously doubt whether the life-is-meaningless formula, with its implied appeal to healing meaning from beyond, really gets at the essential predicament of American ageric culture. Americans are so active not because life is meaningless, but on the contrary because their actions are so consistently productive of satisfying meanings. Thus the actual predicament of American society, for most of us, is that its lures and eddies are all *too* meaningful.

The segregationist persists in his uphill struggle not because he is struck by the hopelessness and lack of meaning in the world he has known, but because of the very fact that his closed system of human relations was so intensely meaningful and satisfying. The professional super-patriot wants to hang the premier of Marxist Cuba not because nothing makes sense, but because his system of sealed and certified Americanism means so much to him, and he wants to keep it pure. What is usually wrong with us, Jonathan Edwards suggests, is our disposition to find life as we know it all too meaningful; what is wrong with us is the idolatry we commit when we find powerful meaning within a "private system."[30]

But now we can see that Tillich has hold of a compelling truth, after all; it is his emphasis that is wrong. These two conditions— meaninglessness and glad, idolatrous commitment to limited meanings short of universal being—are not so very far apart. To phrase our theology in terms of meaninglessness, however, is to overstate the plight of natural man, as we have seen, and also to focus upon the less revelatory aspect of it. To talk about meaninglessness really tells us little about the actual shape of sin, which occurs at the point where we substitute positive but limited meanings for ultimate concern. It misleads us as to the sources of our salvation, for it suggests, as did the sixteenth-century formulation of justification by faith, that the immanent values of society and culture bear no salvific meaning.

All of this indicates that our theological stance for Christian ethics now requires rethinking that will take into account the "new" anthropology, i.e., ageric man as represented, say, by *homo Americanus*. The choice before us is not that of the theological seesaw in which the elevation of God requires the downgrading of man and culture (or contrariwise, to take a current example, in which the elevation of man requires the death of God). The choice is not that posed implicitly by the formula *sola fide*: a sinful, active self-reliance, versus a virtuous, passive dependence on God.

Man's problem is not that he is naturally strengthless and finds no meaning in life, but on the contrary that he is too strong, too able, finds too much meaning on interesting side journeys. "Sin" does not consist in worthlessness and depravity, but in idolatrous, wrongheaded worthwhileness and dexterity. Man's predicament does not consist in helplessness, but of being diverted from his active pilgrimage toward fulfillment by the immensely tempting small, limited areas of life which surround him. Saving grace is not "strength" of some kind, for we already have plenty of that, both physical and moral; grace is direction, a sense of time and terrain, a comprehension of value, the gift of moving into the presence of God and the others, and of moving with the others toward the future.

VII

A SUGGESTED STANCE:

PROMISE AND FULFILLMENT

THE STANDARD ALTERNATIVE, when one realizes the inadequacies of justification as stance and standard for Christian ethics, is some form of the Augustinian and Catholic stance which stresses *caritas* or the ability to love. Love, after all, is the theological virtue most like action itself in its inner fiber. Logically it might be, then, a more congruent and telling standard of excellence for measuring the quality of ethical action in the ageric culture than faith. Faith, as we have just seen, is often taken as a passive or static or intellectualistic dimension of religion, even if wrongly so. Love, as well as faith, can represent the divine initiative and the giftlike character of grace. Love also will not hear of the exclusivity and cultural isolation that the formula *sola fide* has not prevented. Love, unlike faith, does not easily make common cause with notions of election and right belief; it is in its inmost nature an outgoing, neighbor-regarding phenomenon, rarely confinable within ecclesiastical perimeters. (Faith in the Western world has often been a source of sharp division: the Reformers would expel for wrong faith, and in rare cases, justify execution.) Ours is a pluralistic, secular society, in which the ancient hegemony of the church has been replaced by competing centers of value, both churchly and worldly. Manifestly, love as stance offers a basis for common ethical discussion in such a society where faith can never hope to. It is not surprising, then, that a number of contemporary theologians, among them Nels Ferré and Paul Tillich, have made love the basic principle of personal and social ethics, especially in the sense of *agape,* which points to a source beyond the finite, brings forgiveness and acceptance, and drives toward reconciliation.

Yet love as stance in its turn opens up a nest of problems for the ethicist. The word itself has been badly battered by two groups, sentimentalists and biblical theologians. The former have made love over into an all-available triviality. The latter have made it into an eschatological impossibility. Moreover, despite the warnings of biblical scholars that love and justice are part of the same continuum of divine qualities, there is an inevitable tendency in temporal affairs to separate them and contrast them as almost opposite qualities.

More decisive than these semantic problems is the question whether love is really the most *basic theological notion* for the purposes of the ethicist. Love, it seems to me on consideration, is not itself the ultimate goal of human life, but rather the qualitatively highest mode of reaching it. This goal itself, I should say, is what the older theologians called *redemption,* which Jonathan Edwards designates as "the greatest of all God's works of which we have any notice, and . . . the end of all his other works."[31] Salvation would be another term for this goal. Whichever term we use, what is entailed is the bringing of man "back" from his present state to a promised fulfillment of some sort—a restoring of his sonship to God which he does not now enjoy.

The twentieth-century redemption or salvation of man, I now propose, is best of all captured in the idea of *wholeness.* This is what the Gospel brings man "back" to or saves him for, to our way of reading our plight. Wholeness is a better word than redemption or salvation, for it is free of the unacceptable implication that man's destiny under God's grace is transport to some kind of superterrestrial realm. It permits us to proceed with the assumption that man is to reach his end under God genuinely and actually in *this* monopolar reality, the world of time and space, which is the only reality we know. Perhaps his fulfillment will continue in some fashion *beyond* this reality, but it includes realization *at least* in the present world. We really do not have to justify our use of the word "wholeness," for it is closely related in any case to the word "salvation," as is exemplified in the familiar German word for salvation, *Heil,* a cognate of the English *whole.* Our words *salvation* and *safe* have found their way through Old

French and Middle English from the Latin *salvus*, safe, healthy, whole, which is related to the Greek *holos*, complete, entire, the Old English *hāl*, inviolate, intact, and the Sanskrit *sarva*, unharmed, entire.[32]

We can distinguish two tendencies in these roots. Some of them point toward the idea of *safety*, others toward the idea of *completeness*. Some, such as the Latin and Sanskrit, contain both ideas. Evidently the idea of salvation can go in either direction, depending on the circumstances. It can be thought of as a rescue from danger, or it can be thought of as the restoration of one's fullness. Until the Enlightenment, I believe, the primary meaning of salvation in Christendom was *safety*, the deliverance of man from sin and mortality, and especially his rescue from an evil, temporal world, conceived as a transitory realm of suffering. This medieval meaning has been echoed with decreasing conviction in modern times, as in the frontier American revival. But with the full discovery of human self-sufficiency in the eighteenth century and the related discovery that nature could be bent to man's will, this older aspect of salvation begins to lose its relevance, especially the idea that the Gospel comes to extricate man from the miseries of the temporal world and assure him of safety in eternity.

At the same time, the modern world brings with it a new plight. Man's predicament is no longer fear of the world accompanied by the conviction that he will have to be translated into a changeless realm to know his end. His fear in modern times is his own freedom and power, which he has consistently used, among other purposes, to *divide him against himself*, both in his personal psyche and in his social groupings. Furthermore, he is endlessly assailed from without by the desirable features of life in the world, each of which competes for his full allegiance. Modern man's plight is that he is *less than complete*. He is divided against himself: there is a cleft in his psyche and there are fractures, conflicts between groups, as in national, racial and other social tensions. He is pulled in various directions by the competing challenges, lures, and prizes of this world. In other words, man no longer needs "safety" so much as he needs "wholeness," restoration of a solid front. And love, we can now see, is the *way* to wholeness. It is the first of all actions, the criterion of human conduct and of every effort to restore the completeness to man. It is the "awakening and positive fulfillment of humanity" (Karl Barth).[33]

In Genesis 3, the account of the fall, man is pictured as having sundered his defining relationships, those which make him what he is and which tell him who he is—those that make him wholly human, we might say. I see three of these fundamental defining relationships in the Genesis account of creation and fall. All are intimated in a single two-verse passage:

> Then God said, "Let us make man in our image, after our like-
> ness; and let them have dominion over the birds of the air, and
> over the cattle, and over all the earth, and over every creeping
> thing that creeps upon the earth." So God created man in his own
> image, in the image of God he created him; male and female he
> created them (Genesis 1:26-27).

Man is pictured here as enjoying wholeness only when he is open in three dimensions: to God, to men, and to nature.

The first dimension which defines man is his creation in the image of God. I have already outlined my belief that this determination of man refers to his initiative, freedom, and dexterity, his structure as self-reliant and active.[34] These are the characters of God which man reflects in his own being. He is like God in that he can initiate and act. Orthodox Christian theology was right in insisting that the first doctrine of the faith to be dealt with is the doctrine of God. To know ourselves as we really are requires the knowledge of God. Any doctrine of man that omits the knowledge of God risks underestimating the possibilities of man. That is why a theology that takes the slogan, "God is dead," too literally is likely to produce bad anthropology as well as a missing doctrine of God. God is not dead in the twentieth century, though older ways of knowing him may be. God is not in heaven beyond, to be sure; he is known in man. And man is most man when he knows that he reflects God in his acts and being.

Thus openness to God is the first defining relation for man.

The second relation follows from the first and tells of man's place in nature. He is to dominate it. If man is like God in his initiative and ability, he is to display it by ruling over and caring for nature. This is, however, only the outer side of man's reflection of God in his own person. He is God's agent and mirror image as scientist and technologist, as student and transformer of the world; he is truly representing in his deeds, by reflection, what God is like.

But there is a third, fuller reflection of godlikeness in man, and this is seen in man's calling to live with himself, symbolized in the words "male and female." Man's initiative, freedom, and dexterity are deployed as *imago dei* in two directions: (1) *outwardly* in dominion over nature; (2) *fully* in encounter and communication with other human beings. (I say "fully" in the second case rather than "inwardly" to avoid the existentialist fallacy. There can be outwardness without inwardness, but there can be no inwardness without outwardness. The essentially human is both, rather than pure inwardness.) Man is like God in one way when he boldly acts to transform nature. But he is like God in another and higher way when he boldly acts to realize solidarity and rapport with other men.

For the twentieth century the "male and female" dimension is the culmination of the series. The explosion of "encounter" theology, prompted by Martin Buber's poetic tract, *I and Thou,* and taken up by existentialism and neo-orthodoxy alike, has been in effect a massive commentary upon this single teaching of the Bible. Our problem is not safety but completeness—commonness between men, communication, rapprochement, re-unity. In our century the very model of fulfilled, whole man is man in communication, as evidenced in the universal tendency in Wesley Foundations and Canterbury Houses to swear by the word "dialogue."

In respect of this stress on communication as wholeness, our century has moved away from the Enlightenment. The eighteenth-century ideal was the whole *individual,* the man who could stand alone. Robinson Crusoe was the personification of this ideal as the self-sufficient man who conquered nature. Gulliver is another expression of it as the self-sufficient man who coped with human beings in their societies. The Puritan heroes "wrestled alone with their God," and the human entity contemplated in both Locke and Hobbes is the individual who exists as a prior reality to society.[35]

Despite our emphasis upon dissevered human relations, the fall is a description of man's loss of all three of the dimensions. He uses his autonomy not to reflect the divine lordship in the world but to edge God out. He uses his power over nature not to enter into a fruitful relation with the world, but to exploit nature (the red gullies left by rapacious agriculture are for me the best picture of man's dissevered relation with nature; but the dire possibilities of the Bomb represent this for most others). Finally, he uses his specialness as a person, his uniqueness (symbolized in the complementarity of male and female) not to add to and complete humanity, but to divide and conquer.

Salvation is the reopening of these relations. It is the restoration of openness to God, nature, and man. It is re-creation. But the distinct contribution of the New Testament to the picture is to tell us that what is restored is more than a simple return to the "way things were" before the fall. In Jesus Christ the restoration brings higher possibilities than we had in the first place. Jesus Christ is the man who reflects the image of God aright, which means he is something new in history, something we never had around before. But we must not yield to the old anthropology in picturing this man in whom God really lives. We must not picture Jesus as a passive, effeminate type. He is rather the prototype of free and autonomous man, who throws off tradition, defies convention, and takes matters into his own hands—as a way of serving God. As such, he is the man who personifies human mastery over a beneficent nature (the story of the transformation of water into wine at Cana is a *locus classicus* of this dimension).[36] Finally, Jesus' raising of the neighbor to the level of love of God[37] and his offering of love as the criteriological mode of communication between neighbors are the restoration and renewal of the third dimension, between man and man. What is restored in Jesus Christ, in brief, is the glory of God reflected in the fullness of man's humanity. God has created us and placed us in the world, says Calvin "in order to be glorified in us." And Barth, commenting on this remark, holds that "in man God is to be glorified. . . . God does not will to be great and glorious apart from man."[38] But this means that God is glorified only as man is wholly man, and to be wholly man means at least the filling out of these three dimensions of existence:

(1) A man is not a man unless he lives as *imago dei,* unless his lordly freedom and initiative are used to witness to the God who is the fountain of freedom and initiative. Man can thus never dispense with "the difficult word 'God' " or its equivalent; he can never translate all that is implied in the *imago dei* into ideas or models "exclusively from the area of human experiences which do not require transempirical language."[39] We can replace the limp passivity of older theology with a stout doctrine of human ability and still confess the origin of this human ability in God. An anthropology which does not present man as active and autonomous is subhuman, but an anthropology which regards man's activity and autonomy as self-explanatory is elliptical and opens the way for the distortion of these gifts into pride and arrogance. The stronger man becomes, the more we must refer to God to depict him.

(2) A man is not a man unless he is in controlling intercommunication with the nature out of which he comes and to which he will return. If he fails to control nature, he is defeated at the whole project of humanity, for nature will intimidate him, starve him, keep him so pressed he will never have time to reflect or love. Thus man cannot be truly human without technology. On the other hand, to have dominion is not to exploit. When man moves from the status of protective lord over nature to its tyrant, nature flees from him, strikes back, and frustrates him. Thus man must always, even as lord of nature, remember that he is part of nature, after all.

(3) A man is not a man unless he is in communication and community with other men—not merely "responsive" relations with them but initiatory relations which evoke response. Alone he is unwhole, incomplete. He finds himself only as he finds commu-

nity. "The humanity of each and every man," Karl Barth tells us, "consists in the determination of man's being as a being with others, or rather with the other man." This sort of being is the fullest implementation of man's calling to reflect God; in fellowship "he corresponds to his determination to be God's covenant-partner."[40] This fellowship is not that which submerges the person but that which calls on the person to fill out the fullness of the community with his own uniqueness.

Man's way to this end of wholeness has been commonly treated in the Bible and in Christian theology as a *pilgrimage*. He is pictured as having originally been promised wholeness, as having frustrated this promise through historical misuse of his freedom and power, and as having this promise restored to him in Jesus Christ. This idea of movement across time and space to fulfillment is concretely illustrated by the travels of the children of Abraham or by Augustine's use of the passage of time to illustrate the purposes of God in his *City of God*. Such figures as Francis of Assisi and Bonaventura understand man's destiny as including a journey through the temporal world toward the goal of return to God or reunion with him. By the seventeenth century, the part of the journey which took men through the spatio-temporal world had taken on much more positive significance. If earthly existence was not yet to be counted as something valuable in and of itself, yet it is still enhanced with a new attractiveness—as a time of active preparation (rather than of resigned endurance) for the reward beyond time and space. *Pilgrim's Progress* is an allegory which deliberately makes use of the metaphors and parables of a journey, Bunyan tells us, to get at the truth of "the way and race of saints" and "their . . . way to glory."

> This book it chalketh out before thine eyes
> The man that seeks the everlasting prize;
> It shows you whence he comes, whither he goes;
> What he leaves undone, also what he does;
> It also shows you how he runs and runs,
> Till he unto the gate of glory comes.

"This book will make a traveler of thee," Bunyan assures his reader, "yea, it will make the slothful active be." And here we feel the spirit of the new age, the age of the Puritans. They are not fully moderns, but they take more stock in the earthly journey than their medieval forebears. "This life is the time of striving, of running, of acting," the Puritan preacher John Preston announced, even if "it is not the time of being rewarded." In an analysis of Preston's political sermons, Christopher Hill shows that there is a strong sense in them of divine providence *as enacted through human agency*. Preston's outlook is to seat the pilgrimage firmly in the world of history and politics. He is the opposite of an escapist. Man's journey is through a world the operations of which are much more integral to the divine purposes than men had formerly realized. As before, the end and reward of life lies beyond, in eternity. But the world takes on dynamic substance in that it is the arena where men may make their response to the will of God.[41]

The notion of man as journeyer is not peculiar to the Judaeo-Christian tradition, of course. The Greeks thought of man as traveler, too, although Homer's Ulysses is more a wandering warrior than a pilgrim. In the contemporary world, also, the secular alternatives to the pilgrim are abundant. Bunyan's allegory of Christian seeking Zion is replaced by the various models of the historians of progress, the economists, and the evolutionists. Now man's movement through the time-space continuum is not a preparation for something else; if there is any fulfillment at all for him, it comes to him on the way, not after the journey is over.

One cannot really settle much even if he accepts this secular view. For its terms, even within the limitations of a finite journey through space and time, permit an immense range of possibilities. At one end of the scale are nihilists, who argue that life is meaningless and has no goal, hence no fulfillment. At the other end are those humanists who argue that life is at least *meaningful* in the spatio-temporal realm, and that maybe even "meaningful" is too weak a term, for men living as human beings can know, in a sense, blessedness. The meaning of life may even transcend death, for some of these. In the center are most modern men, inhabiting that zone in which both the despair of the nihilist and the optimism of the idealists and theists are rejected. Most men

find life to be neither meaningless nor productive of final ends—
but rather reasonably well furnished with small meanings and in-
cidental ends. Life is neither barren of goals nor decisively organized about a final goal. It is, instead, a mosaic of tidbits, small
morsels of meaning and value. Life is a process of browsing or
moving around in a very small orbit.

One can accept the reality of the modern world without accepting either fate—the denying of fulfillment or the wasting of
human beings upon the limited fulfillments we have just spoken
of. James Joyce's *Ulysses* is an impressive attempt to think of
man's journey in larger terms, yet to do so by way of the real
artifacts of man's life in space and time. This novel tells the story
of one day in the life of one Leopold Bloom—a day fixed in time
(June 16, 1904), and space (Dublin). It is the story of Everyman
told with the concrete bits and pieces of reality that made up the
life of one man. It aims to speak of man as "fabulous voyager,"
and to evoke the mystery of "the path of Everyman through
space and time to infinity."[42] Joyce did not write as an exponent,
in any professional sense, of Christian doctrine. Yet the Christian
origins of his vision are everywhere latent. And this difficult novel
in its very style affords us a clue. One of the distinctive features
of the Judaeo-Christian faith now, as ever, is to insist upon the
reality of the promise of fulfillment out of which man lives; but it
must now find the ingredients of that fulfillment, at least provisionally, in man's journey through time and space. Man is still to
be depicted as a pilgrim, we are saying, even in the modern
world—indeed, he may all the better be so depicted, with the aid
of the understanding of reality proper to our times. Man's end is
wholeness, and he wins it in his finitude, his temporality and his
spatiality. Time and space no longer have to be dropped, in the
end, to point to what man "really" becomes. He finds himself in
the midst of time and space.

The Judaeo-Christian faith, then, offers a distinctive understanding of what is happening to man: he is moving from *promise* to *fulfillment*.[43] While the Christian will place no limits on the
process and will not say that it does not continue in some transcendent fashion after death or beyond the world, he will be

prepared to state his case for the purposes of Christian ethics in terms of spatio-temporal movement to fulfillment. Man's promise is unfolding in history, not just the sacred history of biblical theologians, but in the history of the struggle to be human, which includes all of history. If the realization of this promise enters history through the appearance of Jesus, the appropriation of it continues in the acts and deeds of men.

We may illustrate by noting the partial implementation of human wholeness in the American political ordeal, particularly as this process was envisioned by Abraham Lincoln. In speech after speech Lincoln refers to the Declaration of Independence and the Bill of Rights as the instruments which unfold a promise from God, as translations into political reality of the biblical hope. In the campaign for the Senate against Douglas, Lincoln spoke at Springfield of the Bill of Rights as a criterion "for free society, which should be familiar to all, and revered by all; constantly looked to, constantly labored for, and even though never perfectly attained, constantly approximated, and thereby constantly spreading and deepening its influence, and augmenting the happiness and value of life to all people of all colors everywhere." This political implementation of freedom, in other words, is a promise on the way to fulfillment, a promise put in definitive form for American society in the Declaration of Independence, which Lincoln calls "that which gave promise that in due time the weights should be lifted from the shoulders of all men, and that *all* should have an equal chance."[44]

Lincoln makes it clear that he regards this political promise as a fruit of the divine favor, and that the frustrations of it Americans have known are to be regarded as rebellion against God. "It is the duty of nations as well as of men to own their dependence upon the overruling power of God," he said in 1862. "May we not justly fear that the awful calamity of civil war which now desolates the land may be but a punishment inflicted upon us?" At the same time, Lincoln does not see man as the passive instrument of the divine. Rather men are what we might call ageric witnesses to the promise, participants in their own fulfillment. "All creation is a mine," Lincoln wrote, "and every man, a miner." Man was to make use of "his physical, moral, and intellectual nature" to participate in the unfolding of God's promise.[45]

Not that the American experience captured the whole of the divine promise, or even realized that part of it open to its vision. This is only God's "almost chosen people," to take a phrase from Lincoln's address to the New Jersey state senate in 1861.[46] In any case, every increment of realization only presents us with a further challenge because the more human we are, the more human yet we can become. The political equality offered in the American dream is but a gain, a fragment of the divine promise to man. But its unfolding illustrates in concrete terms the unfolding of that fuller and larger promise told in the Gospel, by which man will realize his whole humanity. Human beings are in general God's "almost chosen people," capable of advancing into new, restored humanity, which is perennially good, but not good enough.

NOTES

1. H. Richard Niebuhr, *The Responsible Self*, pp. 43-44; Ramsey, *Basic Christian Ethics*, xii; Paul Lehmann, *Ethics in a Christian Context* (New York: Harper & Row, 1963), pp. 25, 45, 124.

2. Brunner, *The Divine Imperative*, p. 116; Lehmann, *Ethics in a Christian Context*, pp. 45, 124.

3. The "Egypt and Exodus" theme appears in Ramsey's *Nine Modern Moralists* (New York: Prentice-Hall, 1962), and the in-principled love theme in many of his writings.

4. *The Responsible Self*, pp. 43-44, 55, 60, 61, 67.

5. *Ethik*, p. 6.

6. *Theologische Ethik*, I, ¶¶ 173, 175, 180.

7. Above, p. 18.

8. See Rauschenbusch's *Christianity and the Social Crisis* (New York: The Macmillan Co., 1907) and *Christianizing the Social Order* (New York: The Macmillan Co., 1912).

9. See the criticisms of Luther in George Henri Tavard, *Holy Writ or Holy Church: the Crisis of the Protestant Reformation* (London: Burns & Oates, 1959), pp. 81, 84, 89.

10. *Nine Modern Moralists*, p. 2.

11. Above, p. 9.

12. *The Cost of Discipleship*, tr. R. H. Fuller (New York: The Macmillan Co., 1948), p. 37.

13. Charles Grandison Finney, *Lectures on Revivals of Religion* (Cambridge: Belknap Press of Harvard University Press, 1960), p. 207. In his study of religious groups in Detroit, (*The Religious Factor*), Lenski found

strong persistence of the orientation which values hard work among white Protestants. The dominant value pattern of American society, says the sociologist Talcott Parsons, is "instrumental activism," which comes from moral and religious orientations that "derive directly from Puritan traditions." "Youth in the Context of American Society," *Daedalus*, Winter, 1962, p. 100.

14. G. E. Aylmer, *A Short History of Seventeenth-Century England* (New York: Mentor Books, 1963), pp. 142-43. The juxtaposition of *sola fide* and election occurs, for example, in the theology of William Perkins (d. 1602). Christopher Hill, in a study of Perkins' thought, links his "obsession with the doctrine of justification by faith alone and the powerlessness of fallen man" with "his conviction that there is a predestinate minority of the elect who can be quite sure of their election." Christopher Hill, *Puritanism and Revolution* (New York: Schocken Books, 1958), p. 217.

15. The frontier spirit is best exemplified for this point in the evolution of Cumberland Presbyterian doctrine, which finally moved to an open and avowed advocacy of synergism or cooperation between God and man, this replacing the doctrine of inability of the Westminster Confession. See, too, the essay of the youthful Dietrich Bonhoeffer, "Protestantismus Ohne Reformation," in which it is claimed that "God has granted American Christianity no Reformation. . . . Christianity, for American theology, is still essentially a matter of religion and ethics." Dietrich Bonhoeffer, *Gesammelte Schriften* (Munich: Kaiser Verlag, 1958), I, 353.

16. "Concerning Efficacious Grace," *The Works of President Edwards* (Leeds: Edward Baines, 1811), VIII, 454. Cf. Thomas Anton Schafer, "Jonathan Edwards and Justification by Faith," *Church History*, XX (December, 1951), pp. 55-67. Edwards continues, of course, to manifest the older anthropology in many respects, as in his deterministic view of the will, which his successors rightly regarded as in need of humanization.

17. *Institutes of the Christian Religion*, tr. Henry Beveridge (London: James Clarke & Co., 1957).

18. Karl Holl, *The Cultural Significance of the Reformation*, tr. Karl Hertz *et al.* (New York: Meridian Books, Inc., Living Age Books, 1959), pp. 32-33, 160.

19. Friedrich Schleiermacher, *The Christian Faith*, tr. from the second German ed. (Edinburgh: T. & T. Clark, 1928), pp. 13-17.

20. Simone Weil, *Waiting for God* (London: Collins Fontana Books, 1959), pp. 146-47, 149.

21. Karl Rahner, *Nature and Grace*, p. 110.

22. Nietzsche's remarks are cited in Werkmeister, *Theories of Ethics*, pp. 209, 219. Edward T. Hall, *The Silent Language* (New York: Doubleday & Co., 1959), pp. 178-79.

23. The two-realms doctrine as applied against the peasants is found in Luther's treatises, "Against the Robbing and Murdering Hordes of Peasants," and "An Open Letter Concerning the Hard Book Against the Peasants," *Works of Martin Luther*, IV, 248-54 and 259-81. But we should always keep in mind such countervailing moods as Luther's healthy, life-affirming criticisms of the ascetic life of the monasteries.

24. A representative result of the Protestant separation of temporal life, as province of Law, from spiritual life, as province of Gospel, is seen in the persistence of slavery in the Protestant South. In 1727 the Bishop of London wrote slaveowners in America: "Christianity and the embracing of the Gospel does not make the least alteration in civil property. . . . The

freedom which Christianity gives is a freedom from the bondage of sin and satan . . . but as to men's outward *condition,* whatever that was before, whether bond or free, their being baptized and becoming Christians makes no manner of change in it." Quoted in J. O. Buswell III, *Slavery Segregation and Scripture* (Grand Rapids: Wm. B. Eerdmans, 1964), p. 31.

Among those who have criticized the Reformers' tendency to give the secular realm over to Law is Karl Barth. When they separated justice and love, and ascribed governance of temporal society to Law and not Gospel, they departed from the Word of God. "We can neither overlook nor take lightly this gap in the teaching that we have received from the fathers of our church—the lack of a gospel foundation, that is to say, in the strictest sense, of a Christological foundation." "Church and State," in *Community, State and Church* (New York: Doubleday & Co., Anchor Books, 1960), p. 104.

25. Christopher Dawson, *Religion and the Rise of Western Culture* (New York: Doubleday & Co., Image Books, 1958), pp. 100, 104-106, 113. Luther's great interest in education should be kept in view for balance. See his sermon, "On the Duty of Sending Children to School," and his letter to German municipal officials on behalf of schools, both in *Luther on Education,* tr. F. V. N. Painter (Philadelphia: Lutheran Publication Society, 1889); R. Newton Flew, *The Idea of Perfection in Christian Theology* (London: Oxford University Press, 1934), p. 339.

26. *Church Dogmatics,* III/2, tr. G. W. Bromiley *et al.* (Edinburgh: T. & T. Clark, 1957), p. 184.

27. Viktor E. Frankl, *From Death Camp to Existentialism,* tr. Ilse Lasch (Boston: Beacon Press, 1959), pp. 108-109.

28. Paul Tillich, *Systematic Theology,* III (Chicago: University of Chicago Press, 1963), pp. 227-28; *Systematic Theology,* I (Chicago: University of Chicago Press, 1951), p. 201; *The Courage to Be* (New Haven: Yale University Press, 1952), pp. 142-43, 171.

29. *Systematic Theology,* III, 231-35. A position related to Tillich's is that of the advocates of "dehumanization" as model of plight, who contend that "technology," usually characterized as "demonic" and consisting of "vast impersonal forces," is depersonalizing modern man and making a wasteland of his society. D. L. Munby, in his *God and the Rich Society* (London: Oxford University Press, 1961), exposes the imaginary, romantic character of some of these fears and argues that modern technical society offers possibilities for a humane style of life never dreamed of in the past.

30. Jonathan Edwards, *The Nature of True Virtue* (Ann Arbor: Ann Arbor Paperbacks, University of Michigan Press, 1960), pp. 77-78, 86.

31. "A History of the Work of Redemption," *The Works of President Edwards* (New York: S. Converse, 1829), III, 426.

32. Cf. O. R. Jones, *The Concept of Holiness* (New York: The Macmillan Co., 1961), p. 89: "It seems to me that 'wholeness' understood in a special sense, could be used as a substitute for 'holiness' in many contexts. . . . G. B. Stevens tells us that . . . 'in the Christian system Godlikeness signifies *completeness of life.'* "

33. *Church Dogmatics,* III/2, p. 282. Tillich says that love seeks "reunion of the separated" and that the moral act aims to restore man to personhood and community. *Morality and Beyond,* pp. 18-19, 40. Lehmann's view is that Christian ethics aims not at morality but at "maturity." *Ethics in a Christian Context,* pp. 16-17, 54.

34. Above, p. 53.

35. Hill, *Puritanism and Revolution*, pp. 381-82.

36. Augustus Neander sees Jesus' miracle at Cana not as wizardry but as a model of the transformation of nature for human good. Jesus *"intensified* (so to speak) the powers of water into those of wine," a substance which is "naturally the joint product of the growth of the vine, and of human labor." Christian ethics has a like task, that of enabling the natural "to produce effects beyond the original capacities." *The Life of Jesus Christ in Its Historical Connexion and Historical Developement (sic)* (New York: Harper and Brothers, 1848), pp. 166-68.

37. Love of neighbor, that is to say, is not a substitute for love of God, but is "like it" (Matthew 22:39).

38. *Church Dogmatics*, III/2, p. 183.

39. Van Buren, *The Secular Meaning of the Gospel*, p. 171.

40. *Church Dogmatics*, III/2, p. 243.

41. Bunyan is quoted from the "Author's Apology" to *Pilgrim's Progress*. Hill's study of Preston is found in *Puritanism and Revolution*, pp. 263-64.

42. Richard M. Kain, *Fabulous Voyager: James Joyce's Ulysses* (Chicago: University of Chicago Press, 1947), p. 17.

43. Both terms have a biblical basis. See P. S. Minear, "Promise," *Interpreter's Dictionary* (New York: Abingdon Press, 1962), III, 893-96; C. F. D. Moule, "Fulfill," *Interpreter's Dictionary*, II, 327-30; Werner Georg Kümmel, *Promise and Fulfillment: the Eschatological Message of Jesus* (Naperville, Ill.: Alec R. Allenson, Inc., 1957), pp. 148, 154. All of these treatments are helpful, but they do not sufficiently relate the divine promise to spatio-temporal fulfillment. Kümmel, in fact, roundly rejects this possibility. James D. Smart makes extensive use of the promise-fulfillment concept to solve the problem of the relation of Old and New Testaments in his *The Interpretation of Scripture* (Philadelphia: Westminster Press, 1961). J. K. S. Reid comments: "It is not to be denied that the Bible records a process in revelation. But the process is not from the less to the more developed but from promise to fulfillment." Time is "the order in which God grants fulfillment to promise. . . ." *The Authority of Scripture* (London: Methuen, 1957), p. 187.

44. *The Collected Works of Abraham Lincoln*, ed. Roy P. Basler (New Brunswick, N.J.: Rutgers University Press, 1953), II, 406; IV, 240.

45. *Ibid.*, VI, 155-56; IV, 236; II, 437.

46. *Ibid.*, IV, 236.

Part Three

THE SECOND LOCUS:

WISDOM

VIII

REVELATION AND KNOWLEDGE

THE STANCE OF Christian ethics, as we have just seen, is a platform which lays out the goal of human action according to the distinctive insights of the Judaeo-Christian tradition. But "insights" are a form of knowledge—a special, rich, significant kind of knowledge, perhaps, characterized not only by breadth and unity but by intensity or closeness of personal touch.[1] Still, we cannot avoid the question of knowledge. Though Christian ethics has as its main subject matter the consideration of human actions, part of its way to competence as guide to action is clarity on the knowledge or insight that goes into its guidance.

Immediately we can narrow the field of our investigation. The distinctive insights that concern Christian ethics are those that shape human action, and those only. Moreover, we are concerned in particular with those insights that shape human action toward wholeness (or toward salvation, to use the equivalent term from orthodox Protestant theology). We are not on the quest of knowledge for the sake of knowledge, but only for that knowledge that can provide our deeds "with a sort of coaching," knowledge that is prepared for saving action.[2] "When we speak of revelation," says H. Richard Niebuhr, "we mean that something has happened to us in our history which conditions all our thinking and that through this happening we are enabled to apprehend what we are suffering and doing and what our potentialities are."[3] In this sense Christian ethics depends for its insights upon revelation. It takes its stand on the distinctive features of the Judaeo-Christian way as they shape and qualify human activity. If we can set down on the basis of biblical exegesis, church history, and theological reflection the meaning of the divine promise in Jesus Christ *for human actions*, we have the basis for a stance.

But we must also point out right away the need to *broaden* the field of investigation as well. The light thrown by revelation is to be focused upon the one subject of human actions. But there are also other sources of light relevant for this subject. This is why our second locus is called "wisdom," in fact, instead of "revelation." An adequate stance for Christian ethics must be based on something more than revelation as ordinarily understood. Vital ingredients come from insights and sources of knowledge that are independent of the usually accepted media of revelation, such as Scripture, churchly tradition, or the Quaker's "inner light." Already in Part Two we have seen that this is so, for even if the ethicist begins with a theological category—salvation, in this case —he finds himself looking to the circumstances and predicaments of men in his own times in order to see just what salvation entails for them.[4] "It is very important that theological articulation be accompanied by empirical perception," Peter L. Berger argues. It is not enough, for example, to have a biblical and theologically oriented doctrine of the Church. "One must also have a sociology of the empirically existent churches. A Christian view of our situation can then emerge from the tension between theological doctrine and sociological diagnosis."[5]

As we will discover more fully in Part Four, we cannot write a single relevant word of "Christian ethics" in the twentieth century without revising our conception of human actions, their scope and possibilities. The very idea of freedom is expanding, irregularly perhaps: sociologists point to whole new realms of social commerce in which American youth are now expected to exercise decision, areas that either did not exist in earlier generations, or areas for which earlier youth were expected to "follow the rules." (The more autonomous, permissive aspects of "getting an education" constitute a leading example.)[6] Again, the scientists who formulated the conventions of the metric system in 1795 provided for only seven orders of magnitude (from milli-, .001 upward through kilo-, 1,000). By 1958 the scope of human activity had raced so far "upward" and bored so far "inward" that new prefixes had to be supplied (such as tera-, 10^{12}, and giga-, 10^9, in the macroscosmic; and nano-, 10^{-9}, and pico-, 10^{-12} in the microcosmic).[7] To discuss "human action" is by all means to speak of something perennial about man, but it is also to speak today of a new kind of man along with what is perennial in his conduct.

Part of the reason for looking so intently at modern man is to seek a reflection of Christian values, for in some ways he is the end product of the Judaeo-Christian tradition. If we are to seek out the distinctive features of this tradition we may find some of them helpfully embodied in the literature and art of our times. In Chapter VII, when considering the appropriateness of "pilgrimage" as formal stance for Christian ethics, we briefly juxtaposed the ancient Greek journeyer, Ulysses, and the Christian pilgrim. We hinted there that a telling description of what is distinctive about the Christian pilgrim, in contrast with the Greek hero, appears in Joyce's *Ulysses*. Bloom, Joyce's pilgrim, gets in an argument at a bar with an Irish "citizen" in an episode which echoes the ancient Ulysses' encounter with the Cyclops. But Bloom acts in a new way. The Citizen hurls a biscuit tin after Bloom just as the Cyclops had thrown rocks at Ulysses. Ulysses sought revenge, shouted back, devised a scheme to maim his tormenter. Bloom on the other hand responds mildly, urging reconciliation. Margaret Church concludes:[8]

> On the surface he comes out rather badly, a laughing stock to all who are present. Nevertheless, his weapon, love, may at last be superior to Odysseus' charred stick.

Joyce is able to point to the distinctiveness of the Christian wanderer, using the materials of his own world as it was daily enacted on the streets of Dublin, in a creative way no theologian could duplicate with biblical and dogmatic materials. On the other hand, Joyce could not have painted his portrait of Bloom without the insights of the Judaeo-Christian faith in his own background.

Christian ethics stands between two sources of insight and is in interdependent relation with each. In primary fashion it is dependent on the conventional sources of and aids to revelation—biblical study and exegesis, church history, and theological reflec-

tion. From these it draws the dominating features of its stance
and deduces criteria for controlling the uses of non-revelational
knowledge. But it is also necessarily dependent on the full range
of secular knowledge—"worldly wisdom"—to incarnate the deliverances of revelation and in some ways to supplement, correct,
and replace our obsolescent, ideological, and incomplete versions
of these deliverances. It is now our task to explicate this interdependence.

1. The expression of the stance in ethical terms.

We have already pointed out[9] that the stance for Christian
ethics is immediately to be taken as an ethical statement and not
as a "purely" theological or "pre-ethical" one. The use of the statement should determine the point. Bonhoeffer makes this useful
distinction: "The problem of Christian ethics is the *realization
among God's creatures* of the revelational reality of God in
Christ, just as the problem of dogmatics is the *truth* of the revelational reality of God in Christ."[10] The concern of ethics is realization for human conduct rather than truth as such—as we were
arguing, implicitly, all the while in our reformulation of the
stance in terms of promise and fulfillment in preference to *sola
fide*. At the very outset, the theological ethicist makes use of the
professional gifts (perhaps his own) of the biblical theologian,
the church historian, and so on; yet his goal is not to aim at
exegetical, historical, or dogmatic virtuosity. Such a goal is diver-
sionary, subsersive of the proper task, which is to frame the
implications of the Gospel for human conduct. Not only the language employed, but the way of thinking must reflect the special
responsibility of ethics and the contemporary challenges offered
by problematical human conduct. "The preaching of Jesus Christ
and his reconciling and redeeming act retains a permanence
which the ethical teaching cannot have," says Philippe Maury.
Though we must not change "one iota" of the Gospel, yet "the
preaching of repentance and of new life in the Spirit, in other
words, the Christian ethic, varies with the times, places, and circumstances."[11]

We will be well guided if we remember that reflective Christian ethics is, after all, but a point of departure for the more concrete responsibility of shaping morality; that reflection in ethics is "an act whereby our deeds are provided with a sort of coaching" (Josiah Royce). To remember this concrete destination of our ethicizing is to guard against opening the "theological gulf" which so often vitiates professional stances. It is a good long distance from a biblically and theologically correct recital of a doctrine of man to concrete ethical-moral guidance on civil disobedience or sexual relations. In practice we often camouflage this gap by calling upon some older worked-out morality. Neoorthodoxy, for example, long depended in large part on the older Social Gospel for its program of tactical social action. The Negro non-violent movement attempted to find an ethical rationale for its action program in older varieties of liberal theology, or even in Gandhian thought.[12] One of the real challenges now for those who are truly interested in developing serious theological bases for Christian action lies at this point, near the headwaters, of transmuting theological and biblical presuppositions into the terms of genuinely ethics-oriented discourse.

2. The usefulness of worldly wisdom in modifying the stance.

But more is involved than putting the stance into ethical terms and moving it closer to the point of departure for the concrete situations of morality. A more thorough kind of modification, based on decidedly secular realities, must now be considered. It is well enough to begin our ethical reflection where neo-orthodoxy did and confess: "The point of departure for Christian ethics is not the reality of one's own self, or the reality of the world; nor is it the reality of standards and values. It is the reality of God as He reveals Himself in Jesus Christ."[13] The reality of God, however, as He reveals Himself in Jesus Christ is not a monolithic reality. The scope of the Gospel, and so of our theological stance and of Christian ethics, is as wide as the varieties of human conduct which need redemption, as wide as the deployment of human beings in their manifold activities. Thus worldly wisdom serves as more than a general communicative medium for the Gospel: it also provides specific embodiment for the stance in the diverse reaches and departments of human activity. Christian ethics must deal with more than a general, one-valued, undifferentiated statement of wholeness. (In the sense I have in mind, a great many "existentialist" statements about man are in this way general.) Christian ethics must deal with wholeness in terms of new ages and various geographical and cultural sectors; it must deal with wholeness in various segments of life, e.g., in race relations, medical practice, sexuality, business affairs, war and peace. We may indeed organize the topic of the relevance of worldly wisdom for expressing the stance by considering the approaches across these diverse fields that certain Christian-ethical treatises of our time represent:

(a) We may speak first of overall restatements of the Christian ethic that aim at re-expressing the meaning of the Gospel for twentieth-century man. A good example, inasmuch as it is both systematically ambitious and also aware of the recent history of secularism, is Thielicke's *Theologische Ethik*. We could also mention the writings of Emil Brunner, Karl Barth, Reinhold Niebuhr, H. Richard Niebuhr, Paul Lehmann, and Paul Ramsey, who in various ways attempt restatements of the enterprise of Christian ethics both in the light of the "new theology" (i.e., neo-orthodoxy) and the altered patterns and styles of twentieth-century life.[14]

(b) We may speak of more focused treatments that expound the meaning of the Gospel specifically in the light of new times— the *kairoi* or dramatic new crises in human affairs. The classical Social Gospel illustrates the massive concentration of Christian ethics upon the dominant problem of its own recent time, economic underprivilege. Such books as Kyle Haselden's *The Racial Problem in Christian Perspective* and Gibson Winter's *The New Creation as Metropolis* point to the inexorable shift of ethical concerns into new times and problems. In each case the data of an age's worldly self-consciousness is used to express and differentiate the meaning of the Gospel for human wholeness: the data of industrial life for Walter Rauschenbusch, the data of a gathering national consensus on race relations for Haselden, the data of urbanization for Winter.[15] There is still too little recognition in Christian theology of the decisive coloration that the "course of human events" imparts to the Gospel.

(c) We may speak of theological and ethical treatises that expound the meaning of the Gospel in view of new space and critical shifts in terrain. The classic example in Protestantism is the corpus of New England Puritan writings, which attempted to convert the Reformed Gospel of Europe into the holy way of life of the New England Commonwealth (e.g., Jonathan Edwards' early *Thoughts on the Revival*). In contemporary Christian ethics H. Richard Niebuhr's *The Kingdom of God in America* is another attempt, and an impressive one that should be taken more seriously, to interpret the Gospel in terms of the American experience. My own *The South and Christian Ethics* is an effort to clarify some dimensions of "wholeness" not only in the light of a suddenly emergent racial revolution but even more specifically in the context of the Southern ethos as background to the prophetic word the church must speak. Geographical directionality places a strong, well-nigh indelible mark on the history of ideas, as certain old watchwords and slogans remind us: "Westward the course of empire," "In Dixie land I'll take my stand," *Drang nach Osten*, and so on. There is a strong tendency in theology, as in other intellectual disciplines, to assume that with worldwide transportation and communication, the differentiating effects of space may increasingly be discounted. This is partly true, but on every hand it is also not true. Hoover and Vernon have demonstrated that crucial "locational factors" persist, for example, strongly influencing the choice of plant sites, despite the leveling effects on terrain of efficient means of transport (rail, rubber, circumferential high-speed highways, piggyback rail freight, and air freight). Factors such as the shape and size of city block patterns, they report, "have become a powerful restraint on factory location." Both nature and the human past must be reckoned with by men who seek fulfillment in the future, and these forces cement themselves into our environment by structuring the terrain over which we move.[16]

(d) We may speak of Christian-ethical treatises that expound the meaning of the Gospel in terms of the various callings, or realms of human conduct. In this field it is especially clear that the ethicist must depend on the knowledge peculiar to the practitioners in these realms, not just for "translation" of what the revelatory source has to say, but also for a filling out or *completion* of what is to be said, a supplying of details and implications for the calling or realm at issue. Some of the writings we have already mentioned also illustrate this aspect of the uses of worldly wisdom, e.g., the books on race relations. We may also point as examples to such recent treatises as Paul Ramsey's *War and the Christian Conscience*, D. S. Bailey's *Sexual Ethics: A Christian View*, or Roger Mehl's *Société et Amour*. In each, acquaintance with one or more disciplines outside the normal scope of theology is necessary to the expression of the stance.[17]

Taking these four aspects of Christian-ethical discourse together, we can see that "social ethics" and its various problem areas, such as just-war theory or vocation or race relations, are not to be viewed as appendixlike practical applications of theology or ethical theory, to be deferred to the end of the process of ethicizing. The consideration of concrete outlets for the stance, i.e., social and personal ethical problems, stands as a high priority item in the construction of a systematic Christian ethics. Our stance depends at once on the insights of theology and the wisdom of the ethos, and proper consideration of the role of the latter cannot be postponed, as is common practice in seminary courses on Christian ethics, to last place.

3. The usefulness of worldly wisdom as strategic assistance.

"If the New Testament gave us a social program, including both ends and means, it would have been out of date long ago," says John Bennett. "Instead it gives us the perspective from which to judge all social programs and it constrains us to find the best possible program in each particular situation." Here, concisely stated, is one of the leading contributions of the Anglo-Saxon world to Christian ethics: the insight that the Gospel extends dynamically "beyond itself" into human affairs, and that human response *as such* (rather than specifically faithful or saintly human response) is involved in revealing it and enacting it. We will consider the character of the enactment itself in the next part, under the third locus, but here it is to be observed that worldly wisdom functions as strategic counsel or "staff work" to proclaimers of the Gospel, pointing to places and events in which the word is taking secular flesh, or about to.[18]

We point specifically to two modes of assistance of this kind rendered the Gospel by worldly wisdom:

First, often we find technical issues interwoven with moral and ethical questions. Comprehension of the former may be necessary to proper decisions about the latter, indeed, even to adequate statement of the issues about which decisions are to be made. Condemnation of nuclear testing on ethical grounds, for example, became more urgent and convincing when previous general moralizing about the horrors of future nuclear wars was supplemented with informed scientific opinion about the deleterious effects of fallout. Implementation of the Gospel's mandate to neighborliness across racial lines obviously owes very much in our time to scientific data suggesting the essential continuity of the so-called races of mankind. That the Gospel independently advocates neighborliness among men, without prompting from the social and natural sciences, we may affirm; but this is in a sense a strengthless claim, for American Christians in fact upheld an opposite, pro-white interpretation of the same Gospel for nearly three hundred years. The original impulse to love of neighbor springs from the Gospel, but the implementation of the impulse, and hence to some degree the enactment of the Gospel, depended upon the *kairos* of secular wisdom.

The importance of reliable data from the natural and social sciences has habitually been underestimated by the proponents of conventional, orthodox Christian ethics.[19] Certain tendencies in neo-orthodoxy have only reinforced this failing, even (or especially) among its younger American devotees, who often presented a notorious ignorance of anthropological data and psychological studies, or lack of interest in the working side of the mass media which they found it so easy to denounce.[20] On the other hand, liberal American churchmen of late nineteenth-century vintage, also represented anew in today's younger clerics and theologues, risked getting into the enervating position of attributing all too much numinousness to science. Such types are likely to do nothing until "all the facts are in"—which, of course, is never; or until "one more survey" of the attitudes of youth is made—which will only indicate the need for yet one more. Or, alternatively, they are prone to stake the whole Gospel upon some nostrum dragged in from the behavioral sciences—role-playing therapy or teaching machines. In any case, their stance is determined on the analogy of a pantograph, that old-fashioned copying machine, with the scientists doing the writing.

A genuine theological stance, it is clear, must uphold the *distinctiveness* of the Judaeo-Christian picture of man's promise, although it must not argue its *discontinuity* from worldly wisdom. It must also allow for its enactment via the media of worldly wisdom without affirming a simple continuity between such wisdom and the Gospel.

In the second place, we often find non-theological wisdom adding, besides technical information to our strategy for ethical action, the weight of *parallel pressure*. This issue is best discussed, perhaps, under the locus of action, since pressure comes from activity in society more directly than from wisdom about society. Still, "knowledge is power" (Francis Bacon). The Christian ethicist presumably has a conception of the wholeness of man that is defensible in virtue of its qualitative distinctness and is hence distinguishable from more or less similar pictures of man that stem from secular wisdom. Yet who can deny the enormous pressure toward a wholeness analogous to that of the Gospel which has been laid upon society by the disciplines of depth psychology and psychiatry? Who can gainsay the benefits to the Christian conception of justice that have issued out of legal decisions in the field of American race relations since 1954? If the proclaimers of the Gospel must insist, rightly, upon the distinctiveness of its promise for man, they must not overlook elements of this very Gospel, some of them fundamental, which may be taking fresh and even superior form in various disciplines of the humanities and sciences.

4. Probing of the ethos in diagnosis of the human plight.

So far, in considering the uses of worldly wisdom, we have assumed that the basic features of the stances for Christian ethics arise straightforwardly out of the regular sources of distinctive insight proper to the Judaeo-Christian faith: biblical exegesis and theology, church history, and the reflective-critical talents of the theologian, all applied to understanding "the Word of God." We have assumed, at most, that various supplementary roles (some of them admittedly crucial) are to be played by secular wisdom. Now a further expansion of the role of secular wisdom must be described.

The ethicist must constantly engage in reconnaissance of the ethos to determine if his theological stance is a genuine remedy for the human predicament. Though his theological and ethical understanding is a vital preparation for this reconnaissance, he must necessarily call upon worldly wisdom to play a leading role to assist him in reading the culture and estimating its plight.

Our method, then, is to begin positively with the Gospel, theologically understood as a promise of wholeness to man. From there we move to the ethos, the conventional way of life, which is, according to the Gospel, ever in need of restoration to wholeness. At this point we attempt to "get the facts," gain descriptive knowledge of the ethos with a view to concrete diagnosis of *its form* of frailty, its own rendering of sin. We reserve the right here to modify our presentation of the Gospel so it will match up with and overcome the predicament at hand, instead of overcoming some other predicament, the fevers of some past age or of some other sector of humanity.

Reconnaissance of the ethos, the use of worldly wisdom to investigate the qualities of damnation plays, then, an indispensable role for Christian ethics at the very heart of stance-defining. We may even prefer to extract this aspect of the second locus

from its logical place, and establish it as the first step, as prole-
gomenon to the whole system. We can do so as long as we are
clear that we can begin with "getting the facts" only by standing
proleptically and implicitly upon a positive theological promise
for man that we will clarify when we take up the first locus of the
system. (I have taught an introductory course in Christian ethics
following this latter procedure for five years, although it has only
been in the last year or two that I have realized what I was
doing, i.e., that my "empirical" introduction, a survey of the
problematical state of the American ethos, was in fact heavily
oriented by a theological stance which I treated formally only
later in the course.) The ethicist will take steps to open his inves-
tigations to every helpful means of studying his culture and society. He will necessarily be an amateur in most realms of analysis,
e.g., psychiatry or cultural anthropology. But he no more need be
a professional in these areas than he need be a successful novelist
to use the work of William Faulkner or John Updike as a part of
his reconnaissance. It is essential that the Christian ethicist be a
professional user of theological and ethical conceptions, which
are valid tools in their own right for studying the human environment. He must not be reluctant to make use of the professional work of natural and social scientists and humanists, so far
as he is able, for filling out and supplementing his own methods
of getting at the facts. He will also select one or more non-theological disciplines—literature, political science, or military history,
for example—in which he works at becoming a knowledgeable
amateur.[21] Because he is a professional theologian and ethicist,
he is not a dilettante; but because he is willing to learn from other
disciplines, he is a better theologian and ethicist.

Taken in its role of dealing reflectively with human action before God, theological ethics can then be seen to stand as an
intellectual discipline in its own right. It does not exist in simple
autonomy, independent of dogmatics (so W. Herrmann), or indifferent to worldly wisdom (so classical neo-orthodoxy). Theological ethics is in communication with both sides, but on the
terms of its own distinctive responsibility, which includes both
clarifying the meaning of culture and existence with theological

truth and filling out the full meaning of theological truth by openness to worldly knowledge.[22] Christian ethics becomes sterile and, in my experience, very uninteresting, if it cuts off either of its two sources of insight: the wisdom furnished by the Judaeo-Christian faith about the promise out of which man moves; and the phenomenological insights about man furnished by the divers realms of worldly wisdom, which become the building blocks in every emergence of the promise into reality.[23]

5. The Trinitarian context of worldly wisdom.

In the final analysis we are to visualize the input of worldly wisdom into the fund of Christian-ethical insight not as an admixture of extraneous knowledge but as a continuation of revelation itself. We take this position for a theological reason. For the Christian, the phenomenon of coming-to-know is to be understood in a Trinitarian context. What is promised originally and creatively by the Father is enacted and renewed among men by the Son, and brought to consummation or completion by the Holy Spirit informing the human spirit. Thus the advent of new wisdom today in the minds and spirits of men may be taken as the continuing manifestation of what has already been promised and made certain of coming in the historic sources of revelation.

Our thought on this point may best be guided by the remarks of Gregory of Nazianzus (329-390 A.D.), the great Origenist and master of allegory. Gregory understands the Holy Spirit as the bringer of completeness to men, the consummation of what is given in principle (Father), and already realized as such (Son). In his Fifth Oration on the Holy Spirit, Gregory thinks of revelation, accordingly, as occurring in a threefold fashion. There were already, before the present age, two stages of the divine disclosure to men—two "covenants," "earthquakes," or "conspicuous changes of men's lives." The first, marked by the Old Testament, was the transition from idols to Law. The second, marked by the New Testament, was the transition from Law to Gospel. But the Law and Gospel point ahead of themselves. (They are self-transcending, as we should say today.) Especially does the latter point ahead to a third earthquake or transition in the knowledge of God. "The Old Testament proclaimed the Father openly, and the Son more obscurely. The New manifested the Son, and suggested the Deity of the Spirit." But now, in this third era, "the Spirit Himself dwells among us, and supplies us with a clearer demonstration of Himself." Thus does God gradually unfold truth to men as they are ready for it. The light is still breaking upon us.[24]

Men must never, then, rest content with the wisdom—sacred or secular—that they have been bequeathed from the past. The human mind-spirit itself is a completing medium of the unfolding of wisdom, and this medium must be accepted by Christian ethics in the widest sense of creativity and venturesomeness. The doctrine of the Trinity is both the gateway to worldly wisdom and the critical principle for appraising and evaluating worldly wisdom. "It can be neither discarded nor accepted in its traditional form," says Paul Tillich. "It must be kept open in order to fulfill its original function—to express in embracing symbols the self-manifestation of the Divine Life to man."[25]

IX

A CRITIQUE OF *SOLA SCRIPTURA*

In Part Two we found it necessary to replace the old Protestant watchword "by faith alone" as stance for Christian ethics on grounds of its defective anthropology. Now we must place under scrutiny the cognate Protestant watchword in the field of wisdom: *sola scriptura*, "by Scripture alone."

In his *History of the Work of Redemption*, Jonathan Edwards is well aware that the history of man's salvation is something more than sacred history. To be sure, this greatest of God's works, redemption, is marked in time by sacred events: the Temple replaced the tabernacle, the new Covenant the old, the throne of David the throne of Saul, the priesthood of Christ the priesthood of Aaron. Yet there are other events in world history that figure in this story—especially those epochal upheavals in human affairs that mark turning points, or "all the revolutions in the world," as Edwards says. Edwards understands that men may gain some knowledge of their own destinies out of these secular crises, and indeed, by means of them, act in shaping their destinies. "Reason teaches," he observes, "that God has given his rational creatures a capacity of seeing him in his works." It is fit that men see God's activity in shaping the course of world events, because they are not only rational, but able to act themselves. They are "capable of actively falling in" with God's design, "of promoting it, and acting herein as his friends and subjects."[26]

Here and elsewhere (*Original Sin, The End for Which God Created the World,* and *The Nature of True Virtue,* to mention three treatises) Edwards seems to depart from Reformed orthodoxy on the subject of man's ability to know. Here he seems to affirm the positive natural capacity in man to know something decisive of himself and of God. But the most powerful and persistent theological doctrine in mainline Protestantism was that man cannot really know God and self on his own and must perforce rely on the Scriptures. Despite what he has just said, Edwards, still a man of his times, dutifully sounds this hallowed Protestant doctrine:[27]

> Nothing else but the scriptures has any pretence for showing any manner of regular scheme or drift in those revolutions which God orders from age to age. . . . How rational, worthy, and excellent a revelation . . . is the Bible . . . a book that the great Jehovah has given to mankind for their instruction, without which we should be left in miserable darkness and confusion.

In Edwards' thought, then, two views of knowledge lie side by side. Through his own Puritan background and from the theology of the Westminster Confession of Faith, Edwards had inherited the Protestant affirmation *sola scriptura*. But he was also the beneficiary, on the other hand, of a gathering new consensus upon the positive qualities of the human capacity for knowledge, mediated to Edwards chiefly through the philosophy of Locke and the science of Newton, both of whom he read carefully. Edwards, in brief, is coached from two sides, one urging the supervening importance of divine revelation in the Bible, and the other encouraging the most forthright expectations of the power of natural human reason. But Edwards wins through, in the clutch, to a third position, best illustrated in his treatise *Original Sin*. Here he asserts a kind of complementarity between the human capacity to know (by observation and reason) and the deliverances of Scripture. Scripture clearly retains its primacy as a criterion of knowledge and as a sort of key to the meaning of history, but Edwards also shows that he is in part a modern theologian by finding a positive role for human capacity. Unfortunately, however, he continues to repeat the isolated doctrine of *sola scriptura*, along with his new position.[28]

The facts are, of course, that the original Reformers had on occasion, despite their watchwords stressing our "nullity" (Calvin), recognized the positive capacities of natural human reason. Discussing a difficult ethical decision made by a nobleman,

Luther remarks that "a good and just decision must come from a free mind . . . by love and natural law, with which all reason is filled." The decision in point "sprang from untrammeled reason, above the law in all the books," and was "so excellent that everyone must approve of it and find the justice of it written in his own heart." Written laws should be tested by reason, Luther adds, "from which they originally welled forth as from the spring of justice."[29] This is not a typical utterance of Luther's. But even if it is only a subordinate theme in Luther's understanding of the problem of knowledge, its implications for ethical thinking are evident. Whatever potency we must attach to revealed knowledge as the basis of saving beliefs, it must be supplemented in some way where ethical matters, rather than purely theological ones, are at issue. But this distinction between dogmatic and ethical uses of knowledge long went unrecognized.

Luther and Calvin were properly suspicious, we might add, of the powers of human reason under the goad of *hubris*—as we should be today in a different context. They were further dubious of the claims to revelatory authority asserted by the Catholic proprietors of churchly tradition, who seemed to reject the authority of Scripture; and they were alarmed at the tendencies of spiritualists and some "Anabaptists" to rise above the authority of Scripture on the basis of private or inner "revelations." Despite Luther's occasional tribute to "untrammeled reason" and even Calvin's much more consistent affinity for humanist learning, it is still not surprising that the two Reformers fell upon the Scriptures as a pure fountain of truth to be contrasted with the brackish waters offered by their opponents. Understandably they chose to make their case with the overly pointed formula, *sola scriptura.*

Those of us living this side of Jonathan Edwards can no longer accept the inaccurate and ambiguous formula for saving knowledge, "by Scripture alone," particularly as it bears on the concerns of Christian ethics. Properly reinterpreted, it continues to offer a valid Protestant principle for laying out the scope and direction of theological doctrines, although the rise of historical and literary criticism has raised internal questions that must be dealt with on this point, just as the rise of human autonomy raises questions about the anthropology that goes with justification by faith. But our concern here is not with the Bible as medium of revelation for dogmatics; but instead with the Bible as medium of revelation for Christian ethics, and here, I would suggest, the needed demolishing of pre-critical claims for the sufficiency of Scripture has hardly begun. Christian ethics (more especially, Christian morality) is the field of theological knowledge in which from the Reformation forward, the formula *sola scriptura* has been least applicable. Yet the old assumptions about the sufficiency of Scripture have perhaps found more asylum in contemporary Christian-ethical theory than in contemporary systematic theology, which has at least been helpfully roiled by literary critics and demythologizers.

We can see the persistence of the formula *sola scriptura* or some reasonable facsimile of it at three levels—first, in the ideologies of laymen; second, in the official pronouncements of denominations; and third, in the theories of contemporary Christian ethicists.

At the first level, I am not only thinking of the lay churchman who writes his local newspaper arguing that the Bible teaches segregation, that he believes every word of the Bible, and that the Supreme Court is therefore the anti-Christ. I am also thinking of the "liberal" layman who claims with equal conviction that the Bible teaches integration in a remarkably concrete, twentieth-century fashion. Let me be understood aright. I do not contest that the Bible teaches universal human brotherhood as common sonship under God in a profound and determinative way. Yet it is usually silent when it comes to telling us what this stance entails, for a later age and a different cultural setting, as to applied morality. Worse, in some places where it is not silent, it gives us advice that is manifestly bad if taken literally. Looking for guidance on contemporary race relations, one could easily conclude, from Jesus' interview with the Canaanite woman (Mark 7:24-30, Matthew 15:21-28), that Canaanites are no better than dogs. Indeed, from our point of view, it might even seem that Jesus insults a person of another race. To put it another way, the writers of the Gospels do not understand racial brotherhood as we understand it today. But this episode is not meant for concrete guidance on race relations; its point deals, rather, with Jesus' mission and the possibility of personal response to it, seen in the woman's acceptance of Jesus. As to the theme of race relations itself, I am prepared to defend my own morality over that of the authors and editors of this portion of the Gospels.

Again, I am dubious of the theory of "integration" propounded in Acts 10, which has given rise to such slogans today among liberal churchmen as that we should "love the unlovely." (That, on the whole, is what Peter seems to be doing here.) Other parts of the Bible, to be sure, give us a better understanding; but even more decisively, so do the deliverances of modern secular wisdom with their assurances that there are no "racial" differences worth bothering about and that a better basis for accepting a person of another race than nobly "loving the unlovely" is to realize that we are both, as men, lovable and unlovable. It is possible, indeed, to draw just this latter point from Peter's conclusion: "Truly I perceive that God shows no partiality" (Acts 10:34). But the fact is, Christians did not draw this point until they were prompted by the course of modern events and by the reason and conscience of contemporary secular wisdom, for our current vision of racially integrated society is really quite new. I conclude not that it is wrong, but that other media than the Bible must be accounted authentic sources of revelation for ethics and morality. In the meantime, the misleading formula, *sola scriptura*, persists among the laity, who use it to serve their own ideological interests.[30]

Most of the mainline Protestant denominations have encouraged this misuse of Scripture by freezing the Reformation formula into official pronouncements. The Westminster Shorter Catechism covers the subject as follows:

> The Word of God which is contained in the Scriptures of the Old and New Testaments, is the only rule to direct us how we may glorify and enjoy him. . . . The Scriptures principally teach, what man is to believe concerning God, and what duty God requires of man. . . . The moral law is summarily comprehended in the ten commandments.

Here the formula is put moderately, but even so it misleads us as to the Christian's sources of insight for ethical reflection and moral behavior. The situation is infinitely worse, of course, among those groups which affirm "that the Bible is the very Word of God, inspired and infallible, and inerrant as God gave it, and is to be interpeted in a grammatico-historical manner, whereby the precise meaning of a passage is gathered from the Scriptures themselves." And even the denominations which traditionally have stressed ethical and moral witness have clung in official statements to the *sola scriptura* teaching, as this sentence from one of the Methodist affirmations of faith indicates: "We believe in the Word of God contained in the Old and New Testaments as the sufficient rule both of faith and of practice."[31]

To add to the difficulties, these protests by laymen and denominations and church papers (Baptists are "a fellowship of Bible-believing, Bible-loving people") go largely unobserved and indeed disregarded in morality itself, i.e., in day-to-day decision-making and acting. How many Presbyterians, we might ask, actually practice the following injunction of the Westminster Shorter Catechism as part of their preparation for moral decisions: "That the Word may become effectual to salvation, we must attend thereunto with diligence, preparation, and prayer; receive it with faith and love, lay it up in our hearts, and practice it in our lives."[32] But study after study of the Bible-reading habits of contemporary laymen suggests that the biblical categories are strange indeed to American Christians. It follows that they are neither Bible-loving nor Bible-believing. Thus the inaccuracy of the formula *sola scriptura* for reference to ethics and morality has received an unconscious popular correction (or over-correction) in the widespread tendency to ignore Scripture as a guide to day-to-day living. What is needed is a re-evaluation of the role of Scripture at the reflective, critical level, which may result in asking us to be content with less sweeping claims for it, but which may re-establish Scripture as an effective authority according to its actual value.

What of the views of Christian ethicists, finally? Karl Barth's essay, *Das Geschenk der Freiheit*,[33] contains some remarkable and sensitive descriptions of what the Bible can mean to the "free theologian" who knows himself as such because he lives joyously and relaxedly (*gemächlich*) out of its message. He doesn't come from it with some old or new orthodoxy drummed into him. He has no sense of *having* to live by it, but only that it has been given and allowed him. He hears in the Bible the testimony of the free God and of free men, and as a student of the Bible, he is permitted to be himself a witness to the divine and human freedom.

But what does Barth mean when he speaks of a "free man" before the Bible? The questions of ethics and about the goodness or evil of his deeds have to do "not with his conscience, with the *kairos*, with his opinion-judgments, with any palpable or impalpable natural law or law of history, with any individual or social ideals, and least of all with his own free will," but with "the will, work, and word of the free God!"[34] Here we recognize a familiar picture of man: this is the man of *sola fide*, passive and dependent. To be sure, Barth carefully resists any easy solution to ethics by simply taking the Bible to be a kind of rescuing legal program or a compendium of what is commanded and what is forbidden in the field of human acts. "Holy Scripture is no such charter (*Satzung*)." But the damage has already been done in the restrictions imposed upon this so-called free man before the Bible. Barth helps us by pointing convincingly to the positive resources that the ethicist or theologian joyfully can receive by the study of Scripture. In this respect, his point is well taken. But what he does not allow for is the imaginative appropriation of scriptural insight that is a characteristic of a truly free man reading the Bible—that extension by human inventiveness of the motifs of Scripture into the wisdom of the world, whereby Scripture is made the basis of something new in the moral realm and is given concretion and even correction in the positive learning and other knowledge resources of the men who read it. Barth is a willing and gifted student of biblical criticism and in many other ways he is not to be considered on the same terms as we would the fundamentalists or old-fashioned conservatives. But in the final analysis Barth espouses what amounts to a new, sophisticated version of *sola scriptura* as the one knowledge principle of ethics.[35]

But there is no need to limit ourselves to European thinkers to encounter this persistence of the old dogma of the role of the Bible. It enjoys wide patronage in American theology, too.

For the purposes of the ethicist, Scripture tells us too much—and not enough. It properly is to be regarded as the basis (in a sense to be described in the next chapter) of our stance for ethics, as the leading source of insight about what human wholeness is and the hope men have of attaining it. But the Bible also illustrates its insights with outmoded or downright unacceptable examples of morality, as in some of its recitals of racial encounters or in its espousal of the inferiority of woman. Moreover it leaves large areas of the human problem untouched by its insights, not only at the level of practical morality, but in the more fundamental issues of anthropology. One of these, for example, is the reality of human freedom, a topic that "is not at the centre of Biblical revelation," but rather a subordinate idea to the notion of dependence in the Bible.[36] The Reformation stance, *sola fide,* accepted a view of man that permitted such containment of the human self and accepted the theory that men are dependent on divine revelation in a massive way for knowledge and learning and the ability to evaluate morality. But in the twentieth century our understanding of man is just the inverse. We assume that man's problem is the very ingenuity and proliferation and success of his knowledge. We must start over and look once more for the right role of Scripture, for it is still vital to the Christian-ethical enterprise. We must attempt to rescue Scripture, in short, not from its detractors, but from its publicists in the theological world, and this can be done only on the basis of a view that provides for the sure and steady knowledge of man as ethical creature that is bequeathed us by the advent of worldly wisdom.

X

THE SOURCES OF WISDOM
FOR CHRISTIAN ETHICS

An ethics based on the distinctive stance of promise and ful-fillment offered out of the Judaeo-Christian tradition accords a primacy of some sort to the biblical picture of man's salvation. But this stance itself is dynamic, like leaven, and to be heard, seen, and appropriated, must be sought also in the communities and persons with whom it is concerned. Hence the *community* under divine promise, including the church and the *person* under divine promise, including the conscience or moral sense, stand along with the *Bible* as media of revelation.

Our remaining task is to gain clarity on what the interrelations are among these prospective sources or media of wisdom for Christian ethics.

Albert Peel, in a study of the problem of biblical authority, concisely summarizes the leading "claimants for authority, for the Christian's allegiance" among the conventional media of revela-tion. There are three of them, at first glance not quite the same three that I have just mentioned:

(1) The church—which nourishes tradition and offers a faith-ful community of experience, learning, and reflection that can test "the vagaries, eccentricities, and aberrations of individual inter-pretation."

(2) The written word—which furnishes in Old and New Tes-taments a record, a source of knowledge, a witness to the revela-tion of God to man.

(3) Individual judgment—which appears in many styles over Christian history—as the Quaker's inner light, as the idealist's

reason, as the mystic's immediacy—and becomes the medium by which revelation finally confronts us.[37]

Protestantism has always emphasized the second of these, but a better description of its emphasis than *sola scriptura* might be *scriptura prima inter pares*: Scripture as first among a special set of sources. Peel argues that Protestantism as a rule has also left a positive, though subordinate, place for the other two media, with individual judgment (as reason or conscience) typically relied on secondarily, and churchly authority (understood as the mandatory force of tradition) ranked third. But there have been other permutations in Protestantism. In post-Reformation Lutheranism, one form of churchly authority, understood more as confessionalism or "right doctrine" than as tradition—was considered to outrank individual judgment. Among the Quakers and such spiritualist reformers as Hans Denck, the witness of God to the inner person was placed ahead of Holy Scripture itself. In some present-day American institutionalized sects, such as the Southern Baptists and the Churches of Christ, a formal recognition of the primacy of Scripture is in fact superseded by the right of the ecclesiastical institution.

Since the Reformation, drastic changes have overtaken each of these three claimants for revelational authority, especially in American Christianity. Let us examine some of the changes as they bear on our problem:

1. The church and the new community.

The church is no longer the arbiter of culture it once was. It is no longer the overarching guardian of the salvation and ethical destiny of men it was in the sixteenth century. It now shares the function of commending and evoking wholeness with its associated social and political community. (One reason we have substituted the term "wholeness" for the older term "salvation" is to lay bare the incompleteness of present-day churchly efforts to make men whole.) If morality is now to be guided by sources possessing ethical wisdom and authority cognate with that possessed by the church of the Middle Ages we must look beyond present-day denominations, and indeed past the totality of churchly groups. We must assign this role not only to the church as it persists in its reduced scope, but to the totality of the ethically involved forces in the community. Let us call this totality of forces the "ethically oriented agencies" of the community, and let us call its guidance "community ethical judgment." It is the latter, then, which has now replaced in fact the churchly authority over ethics of the Middle Ages. Tradition or credo or "sound doctrine" of a sort will continue to play a role among the media of wisdom in guiding us to truth and virtue and wholeness; but now it must be the tradition of the community's ethically oriented agencies, the history of the emergence of humanity, and not merely ecclesiastical tradition. Thus the history of justice in our courts, the experience of the educational system, and the cumulative conscience of crusading journalists now figure as elements of "tradition" guiding ethics. The churches will continue to play a large part in their own right as members of this coalition, of course. But churchly hegemony over ethics, even over *Christian* ethics, is gone; the claims of the wider community now stand as the most pertinent transcendent reminder to the individual that his wholeness, though personal, cannot be realized privately.

But we do not want to minimize the role of the church or the explicitly religious community (including both Christian and Jewish subcommunities). This community continues to have the indispensable role of *bearing the criteriological symbols* in this total community of ethical judgment, the symbols of promise and fulfillment. The Christian sector of the community, for example, continues despite its human failings to represent that group of men and women who explicitly define their promise by what they see in Jesus Christ and to base their prospects of fulfillment upon what humanity becomes in him. Both Christian and Jewish sectors have the broader responsibility of nourishing the ancient thesaurus of biblical symbols that go into the vision of man's hope. The vision may come to fruition elsewhere, outside this specifically religious sector, yet it is this sector that functions especially within the fuller community to preserve the living symbols of divine reality whence all promise and fulfillment come.

The religious sector may also, of course, demonstrate the quality of fulfillment as well as preserve the symbols of it. But on this point we will do well to proceed with the moderate kind of claim that Seward Hiltner makes when he discusses the ability of the Christian community to manifest wholeness in the field of sexual relations:[38]

> The meaning and the good of any sex act or relationship are always dependent, in some measure, upon the inner meaning to the persons involved; but the sole ultimate standard for meaning or good is the judgment and love of God, of which the Christian community *may at times* be representative. . . .

The judgment and love of God are for all of the community, and we must not in our reformulation repeat the age-old error of the "sainthood fallacy." The religious sector of the community bears the symbols of promise and fulfillment but its members have no unusual proficiency at saintly living. They are in this respect on the same plane as other men.

Alongside the religious agencies, there are other ethically oriented agencies in the human community. They, too, must be accredited in some sense as authoritative sources of wisdom for ethics, including Christian ethics. If the religious agencies, as we have just seen, have the special function of bearing the prime symbols of man's redemption, what is the special function of the secular agencies? In a word, secular wisdom is the medium in which the age-old symbols engage us today. Scripture and churchly tradition furnish us definitive images, pictures, and themes of wholeness, but we can see, know, and appropriate these only as they take shape in our own world.

One of the central biblical themes we have discussed so far is the notion that man is defined as *imago dei*, that he knows himself to be "like God" in that he is a creature of initiative and activity. Now, we simply do not have the full picture of man-as-active before us unless we take into account the contemporary, secular understanding of what constitutes human activity. Hence to express the meaning of man as *imago dei* for our time requires that we consult the behavioral sciences and other theoretical disciplines that have been especially concerned to understand man as agent in his community and environment. Contemporary accounts of human agency by moral philosophers are another source of this enfleshment and filling-out of the revelational image of man as initiator. Reflective utterances of natural scientists pondering our exploration of the universe add further to the enrichment of the image.

I have found that the theoretical perspective offered by the pragmatic tradition in American philosophy contributes significantly toward giving flesh to the idea of man as initiator. Protracted reading of John Dewey (and, by all means, his recent critics and interpreters) puts hoary theological assumptions to the test and makes us ask ourselves if we must not find new ways of expressing the biblical insights about man.

Theologians are still tempted to isolate the human attribute of activity from other aspects of revelation and anthropology. Because God is eternal and thus prior to man, we may suppose that revelation implies, first, that God approaches man as a "given" to which man reacts without modifying the "given." Because God is eternal and thus posterior to man, we may suppose that man's destiny in God is an end that lies beyond activity and to which the latter is directed. Because revelation implies knowledge of God, we may think of knowledge and consciousness as paths through which the divine may reach us apart from overt activity. Because our very lives, we teach, come from God and do not flow out of our works, we tend to think of our "being" as something more basic, theologically, than our "doing."

While the pragmatist outlook of Dewey and others is in itself riddled with problems, nevertheless it offers a healthy corrective on the role of human activity in response to prior stimuli, and on the general place of agency in describing the self and its destiny.

Every human action is indeed a response of some sort. But it is never a mere reaction to a discontinuous given. It is not, in other words, action after passivity. Stimulus and response overlap and there is interaction between them. If stimulus sets off response, response aims at modifying stimulus. Intelligent action seeks to understand what impinges on us, and more than that, to change it. We do not know God, then, by waiting and acting on the basis of what comes to us, but rather by wrestling with the divine, like Jacob. The "given" that impinges on us is always itself partly defined by the aggressive human act of probing for ultimate meanings. That is why theology is restless, ever questioning the preceding generation's God-ideas. Knowledge of the divine comes to us through the human, as the Incarnation itself should remind us, and what is quintessentially human, according to our understanding of the *imago dei*, is the sense of initiative in communicating and communing.[39]

Similarly, Dewey makes a convincing case that ends, far from existing beyond activity, "arise and function within action." They arise in the course of activity and "give activity added meaning and . . . direct its further course. . . . They are ways of defining and deepening the meaning of activity." Dewey also suggests that it may be futuristic religionists, who see man's end in some trans-temporal realm, and not the nihilists, who have encouraged the twentieth-century conviction that life is meaningless. When we empty present activity of meaning by making it a mere instrumentality, he says, we begin to despise the present and await a future that never comes.[40]

Neither consciousness, nor thought, nor being, may be defined apart from human agency, the pragmatists remind us. "For human beings," says Stuart Hampshire, "to be conscious is to have active intentions." A conscious mind is one "always and necessarily envisaging possibilities of action." The reality of freedom depends on conscious action. "A man becomes more and more a free and responsible agent the more he at all times knows what he is doing."[41] Authentic being, both in the sense of communion with others and in the sense of responsible acceptance of freedom, is based on the "return to experience," a thoughtful Catholic interpreter of Dewey observes. "The very fact that the level of being is the work of freedom makes it a task to be newly begun with the dawn of each day. Since it is attained only by free responsiveness to the Other as it continually comes to presence, the past is no guarantee of its perdurance and even if it lasts it is still to be achieved."[42]

We have explored these contributions of the pragmatic outlook in order to demonstrate the interdependence between age-old theological symbols and secular wisdom. Neither can heal us alone. Sacred symbols, divorced from worldly renewal of their meaning, shrivel in their isolation. Worldly wisdom, apart from theological insights, risks losing the vision of man as *imago dei*, and so risks finally settling for a shallow anthropology.

An adequate account of the contribution from the secular side should not only make a place for the theoretical presentations of ethically oriented forces in the community, but should also provide for the recital of the actual history of ethical movements in the human pageant. During a fifty-year period, for example, from about 1880 to 1935, our society arrived at a provisional consensus, partly at the prompting of the Social Gospel, to grant a better share of the national bounty to the working man. In the period 1830-1850 a national consensus was reached condemning slavery —with a deep rift or cleavage in it represented by the South. In the period 1954-1964 a national consensus emerged which held it unjust and immoral to discriminate against minority groups in publicly owned facilities or even (as the 1964 civil rights legislation held) in "public accommodations." In each of these arrivals at a provisional consensus, we can see historical guidance authoritative for Christian ethics analogous to the revelational reality of church tradition for medieval theology.[43]

But a problem remains: What parts of secular wisdom shall guide us? How do we appraise secular wisdom for its salvation-value? How do we *know* it implements the promise of the Judaeo-Christian faith for man in one instance, and decide that it must be opposed in another? How do we rule out varieties of worldly wisdom—Hitlerism, for example—that destroy rather than fulfill? This leads us to our second historic source of wisdom for Christian ethics.

2. Scripture as *primus inter pares*.

We have already noted the persistence within Protestantism of traditional assumptions about the Bible taken as a medium of revelation. Moderns in the church cheerfully willing, on the one hand, to concede the human origin of the words and thoughts in which the Scriptures are expressed, still have not been able to demolish, for ethics, the age-old assumption of Scripture's supervening authority. The ancient watchword *sola scriptura* is still revered. And yet this reverence is now ideological rather than operational. There is little relation between ethical activity and biblical study for most people in America. But the old slogans supporting the suzerainty of the Bible seem to have paralyzed attempts to rethink the office of Scripture for ethical reflection.

Let us continue to be open, with our Protestant forebears, to the authority of Scripture, but let us take our own affirmation of this authority as seriously for our time as the Reformers did for theirs. This means rethinking the place of Scripture in Christian ethics, and also suggesting an appropriate hermeneutical outlook, or approach to interpreting Scripture, as a source of ethical wisdom.

What, then, of the authority of Scripture for Christian ethics? What the Gospels offer us are accounts of redemption, of the making whole of man. Indirectly the whole of Scripture supports the same end. I propose that Scripture has authority for Christian ethics just as it lives up to this purpose, i.e., as it reveals the gift of wholeness, as it portrays the divine promise for man and really points us toward the fulfillment of it. The Christian reading of Scripture insists that the central representative, bearer, and criterion of this wholeness is the man Jesus Christ. It furthermore insists that this wholeness is characterized by the action and initiative of Jesus Christ as the reflection of the divine in him and that we may "hear" about this redemption only as we act and take initiative, too, performing acts continuous in quality with the acts of Jesus Christ. This understanding, I believe, is a serious acceptance of the authority of the Bible for our times, fully based upon —and the twentieth century cognate—of the Reformation view.

Under this general conception of the authority of Scripture, we can distinguish two aspects, one positive and one negative. On the one hand, Scripture furnishes us the *criteriological symbols* of wholeness. On the other hand, it has the prophetic strength of *disrupting* the forces of unwholeness, and of challenging false authorities, whether sacred, secular, or purely personal, that offer unwholeness instead of wholeness.

On the positive side, the Bible's office of authority for Christian ethics can best be described as criteriological. The Bible is a kind of road map, or a creative source of images that bespeak wholeness-oriented human actions. It "provides us with a perspective; it lays out before us the pattern of the world, and it gives us guidance about the roads on which we are traveling" (D. L. Munby).[44] It furnishes symbols for measuring what is said and done in the world. The symbols range outward around the picture of the whole man of initiative it offers in Jesus Christ. They include the depiction of creation and covenant, the pilgrimage of man through time and space to the promised land, repeated human straying from the divine promise, the rescuing quality of human actions as love. But it is man who does the traveling, and his words and deeds are themselves substantially real alongside of and beyond Scripture. The Bible points the way but does not present valid substantive theories of ethics, then, and much less acceptable moralities, all worked out.[45] To put the implications concisely: Scripture we take to be *constitutive* for major dogmatic or theological themes, *criteriological*[46] for ethical reflection, but *invalid* for morality as such.

But the ethical criteria furnished by the Bible also play a negative role. They not only give us symbols and images of whole man for positive implementation in society. They also have a disruptively creative effect upon worldly wisdom when the latter points away from wholeness. The biblical criteria can render judgment, can become prophetically critical of society, can take away, can question, can destroy. Thus in Hitler's Germany of 1934, the Nazi version of human commonwealth tended toward a glorification of nation and an identification of Germanness with wholeness. The Bible, however, from its *imago dei* teaching forward, through the scorn of the great prophets for false national pride, and down to the teaching of Jesus about the neighbor, brings into question such versions of wholeness. The biblical insistence that men are whole only when they are open to God found expression in the Barmen Declaration, promulgated by a scripturally oriented Christian group opposed to the Nazis. In the present decade, many American churchmen have drawn in like fashion upon the New Testament vision of community to oppose racial segregation both inside and outside the churches.

American Christianity, it can fairly be said, suffers from an absence of this disruptive biblical authority. It is too easy for American communities to fall victim to patently fraudulent leaders who offer counsels of despair or division, often in the name of religion. When the religious symbols are interpreted only in the positive sense, the way is opened for glorification of the status quo with these very symbols invoked as validation or blessing. Thus the great office of Scripture as supplier of symbols of redemption for human community is always to be interpreted in its twofold sense. The symbols point us to wholeness and offer us wholeness. They galvanize social experience and enlist it in the pageant of redemption. But the same symbols also shake up and test society and all its institutions, including the church, in the very name of wholeness. Too, they may question personal vision and put private conscience to the trial, reminding the individual, "disturbingly and redemptively" that his judgment may be fallible.

To set out the office of Scripture, to speak of its authority as criterion for wholeness-oriented human actions, is also to suggest an approach to the hermeneutical problem, or the problem of interpreting Scripture. For Christian ethics, the basis of hermeneutics is a pragmatic affirmation of what we are to expect to find in the Bible: we are to approach the Scripture expecting to find there a picture of man's path to wholeness, the picture of promise and fulfillment.

We can understand this principle in terms of four of the Reformation's guidelines for interpreting Scripture: the perspicuity of Scripture, the interpretation of the obscure by the clear, the focusing upon Christ (*"was Christum treibt"*), and the complementarity of Word and Spirit.

1. The Reformation taught that to eyes of faith, Scripture is perspicuous, plain in its central meaning. One needs no interpret-

ing hierarchy to make clear the merits of Jesus Christ. A contemporary hermeneutics addressed to Christian ethics can affirm much the same thing, though we can no longer be bound by the literal historical meaning. Those who seek wholeness in the twentieth century, like those who "read with faith" in the sixteenth, will find that the Scripture speaks to them of man's promise and fulfillment.

2. Even so, not all parts of Scripture attest with the same lucidity and directness to the story of human wholeness. Following St. Augustine, Luther and Calvin taught that we should interpret the obscure passages by the clear ones. For the twentieth century, we can say much the same. We are to take the gripping, persuasive, compelling images of man the initiator in Scripture and see the other parts in the light of these. To put it another way, everyone who reads Scripture is selective. He chooses certain images and symbols and makes them definitive in treating the rest of the Bible and in outlining his own theology. The Seventh-day Adventist takes one idea, the sanctity of the Jewish Sabbath, and subordinates other portions of Scripture to that point of departure. The Social Gospeler of a half century ago began with the notion of an earthly Kingdom of God. The Southern segregationist often began with the marginal references to ancient tribal distinctions that figure in the Old Testament. In any case, consistency is a virtue of this hermeneutical principle.

3. As a safeguard against the kind of arbitrary possibilities that arise when one is selective in reading Scripture, Luther insisted that what is definitive in Scripture is that which focuses upon Christ (*was Christum treibt*). An ethics of promise and fulfillment says much the same, except that we would rephrase the principle to place more emphasis upon the kind of human actions that are set in motion in the world by the Christ event. In Christ we see man acting for other men, thus reflecting the divine and moving man back toward his true fulfillment. What is definitive in Scripture is that which sets forth man's path to promise and fulfillment.

4. Finally, the Reformers insisted that attention to Scripture is meaningless unless we are enlightened in our inner selves by the

Holy Spirit. Again, we can argue for the same point, though of necessity it must be put in new terms. We have already insisted that a Trinitarian view of wisdom understands scriptural intimations and images to take on new life and freshness in the unfolding of insight and knowledge that takes place historically. If we are confident that the divine speaks anew in human affairs, then we must insist that the biblical message is a lifeless abstraction apart from the communities and persons who are also bearers of the divine. In short, the biblical word takes on life only as it finds its way into the bloodstream of human affairs, political and social developments, and is given flesh in human commerce. The wholeness wrought in Jesus and depicted in the Gospel is realized only as it moves beyond and out of Scripture and into the creation, into the church and community and private consciences of individuals. Just as real community participates in the wholeness definitively embodied in Christ, so "A Christ without His community would be a figment of the imagination" (Karl Barth).[47] Hence Scripture cannot be, for Christian ethics, either an *a priori* or a complete-in-itself authority. Even when it is invested with the considerable office of proffering the symbols of wholeness, that is still only to describe its function as an *initiating* medium. Scripture shares with community and person the claim to be the revealer, in the fullest sense, of wholeness. Scripture is the primary source of those symbols without which we could not recognize promise and fulfillment, but these symbols, in turn, are dead and strengthless until they take on life in communities and selves.

In sum, Scripture is assigned by our conception of authority the rank of first among equally indispensable sources for guiding the enterprise of Christian ethics. It is, to be sure, in a sense one contending authority alongside the collateral authorities of community judgment (which we have considered in the previous subsection) and personal judgment (which we treat next). But where there is conflict over deepseated theological principles, or doubt as to the promise for wholeness of a given stance, as in the German situation of 1934, Scripture is to cast the deciding vote. In hard times it is our refuge, our last resort. Still, at the levels of operational ethics and day-to-day morality, it needs the free competition of the other two media of wisdom.

3. Personal judgment.

Even men who are spiritually dead, according to Thomas Hooker, the seventeenth-century New England divine, "have ability to performe some morall actions; a man hath restraining and preventing grace whereby he is able to wait upon God in the meanes, that so he may be enabled to receive grace." Hooker was quick to supply illustrations of what this ordinary moral sense ought to be able to achieve, even without saving grace. "Why cannot you bestow your bodies to come to Church as well as goe to the Alehouses?" he asked his congregation. "Why cannot you bestow your eyes as well in reading, as in carding and dicing?"[48] Hooker's sermons remind us a bit of that strand of medieval theology which seemed to urge men to "do what they could" even if they did not feel contrition—advice roundly rejected by the Reformers. Yet Hooker's understanding of the natural man was by no means an easygoing one. "Humiliation is the utter nothingness of the soul," he preached, and he thought that salvation, despite intense preparation for it, was still far off for any one who had not thoroughly been broken and disabused of his pride by "the hammer of the Word."[49]

One of the distinctive marks of American moral theology has been the struggle to reconcile two truths about the self, each supported by observation and experience. First, man stands in need of salvation, however we may define it; in his present state he is missing wholeness. Second, man obviously can do moral good without salvation; in his present state he is partly in possession of wholeness. This was Hooker's dilemma and it is ours.

American thought has rejected any solution that would uphold one of these truths about man and exclude the other. It has never really accepted the orthodox Protestant version of the helplessness of natural man. But neither has it shown much toleration for utopian theories, which have been forced to find expression in colonies existing upon the fringes of American society. The American solution to the dilemma has been rather to uphold *both* truths about man, as Hooker did: men can obviously accomplish some moral ends without salvation; but salvation renovates and transforms and provides new possibilities for this previous moral structure. A contemporary expression of the same idea comes from Paul Ramsey. "I affirm that there is some virtue in man's ordinary moral decision," he says, "[yet] I also affirm that no moral judgment is sufficient by nature alone, without in one way or another the saving and transforming power of the agape of Christ." Christian love gives a new sense of what is right to do, yet "Christ does not reign over a structureless world or over men who are bereft of any sense of natural injustice."[50]

Personal judgment is our third positive medium of insight for ethics. Like the other media, it is incomplete in itself. It is a revelatory source in its "sense of natural injustice," to use Ramsey's term, but this sense is not sufficient alone, short of the countervailing insights of community judgment and biblical criteria. We must, however, take note of the expansion over the ages of the possibilities inherent in personal judgment. We live in an age of personal freedom, a time when the ordinary member of society can hope to be given the power to overcome ignorance in the form of education, a time when the mind finds scope uncontrolled by religious or governmental authorities. In other words, the insights of personal judgment today come from persons who enjoy more autonomy than their counterparts of former eras.[51] If the sources of truth we have already considered, the authority of churchly tradition and Scripture, have suffered declining fortunes since the sixteenth century, the source of individual judgment has been correspondingly raised in importance. To be sure, the prevalence of individual initiative is questioned by some today, not because the mind is held in bondage by rulers of any sort, but rather because of tendencies to other-directedness and conformity.[52] This is a ponderable claim; one fears that Heidegger's picture of modern man as lost in sterile everydayness and idle chatter is all too accurate. And we must remember the premise upon which we based our exploration of Christian ethics at the outset of this book, the failure of modern Americans to think ethically, which means in our present terms their failure to use the talents of personal judgment responsibly.

Despite the cautionary nature of these fears about the dearth of reflection, I believe we must, on balance, accord a positive and expanding role to personal judgment as one of our media of wisdom for Christian ethics. Since Kant, no definition of ethics or morality has been able to avoid the ingredient of personal autonomy, for "morality is . . . the relation of actions to the autonomy of the will, i.e., to possible universal lawgiving by maxims of the will." Wisdom depends on "the freedom to make public use of one's reason at every point." All of the wisdom of the past, in fact, must (in Kant's view) pass the bar of autonomous scrutiny: "An age cannot bind itself and ordain to put the succeeding one into such a condition that it cannot extend its (at best very occasional) knowledge, purify itself of errors, and progress in general enlightenment. That would be a crime against human nature, the proper destination of which lies precisely in this progress."[53]

If American citizens do not use their autonomy, freedom, and personal gifts of judgment, it is not because they do not possess them, but rather because these attributes have not been enlisted under the banner of pilgrimage toward fulfillment. But to a considerable extent, contemporary men *do* use their gifts. We could cite the uses of literacy, purchasing power, and above all the sense of injustice among the more disciplined Negro protest groups since 1960. We could cite the display of conscience on the part of an impressive minority of Southern congressmen who broke precedent in 1964 and 1965 by supporting civil rights legislation. If, at the same time, there were rioting Negroes abroad in Northern slums and white "backlashers" decrying civil rights all over the country, we only see the truth of Thomas Hooker's position. Men and their society are not yet whole.

In a sense, the most trying problem presented in the area of personal judgment today is not the general underusage of autonomy and conscience, but a growing, irrepressible *overusage* of these attributes, at least among certain ethically sensitive persons. We are thinking especially of youthful practitioners of the philosophy of non-violence, whether in the cause of racial justice, academic freedom, or nuclear pacifism. Does one's philosophy of non-violence justify breaking a law he considers wrong or unjust? "Yes," we are told. But how does one decide when the law is wrong? All too often, we get the simple answer: "That's a matter of individual conscience."

The view of ethical wisdom that I am advocating does not

allow so simple a solution, for it does not assign unilateral authority to any of the three great media of ethical insight—community judgment, Scripture, or personal judgment (including individual conscience). There are times, to be sure, when we must rely heavily on one of these media to counteract tendencies toward unwholeness in the others. Surely in our own times, the forces of individual conscience, marshaled in the non-violent movement against spiritually inert churches, reactionary social groups, and biblical legalism, have spoken for wholeness. And for this reason we must uphold the right of conscience and its implementation in the form of demonstrations. But it is also true that when any of the media of insight are indefinitely preferred to the exclusion of the others, one-sidedness results that can only issue finally in a new form of unwholeness. Indefinite, protracted reliance upon individual conscience to the exclusion of respect for law, for example, can only produce a distorted and unpromising wholeness that shakes confidence in legal institutions. Full justice for minority groups (to take but one cause in which the non-violent movement has witnessed) must eventually be based upon community support and strengthened by fresh application of the biblical picture of man; it cannot be secured solely by the promptings of individual conscience. And yet it cannot be secured, especially in our times, without a vigorous affirmation of right as delivered to individuals in their consciences.

An ethics of promise and fulfillment attacks the dilemma by pointing to the words "not yet." Men are capable of valid moral judgment, even in their present condition; but they are not yet whole. On their way to wholeness their acts and deeds, made on the basis of personal judgment, can genuinely participate in the struggle. It is when we look at the *person* that we see how much of the pilgrimage of man, indeed, has expressed itself in this category. We think of the contagious drive for human dignity that has ever taken the form of a quest for personal integrity: When the Judaeo-Christian tradition speaks of salvation, we have to look at *persons* even more than at society to find out what it is. Love and freedom are revelatory only when we encounter them, but we can encounter them only in persons. Thus the gifts of personal reflection and action must be accredited a third source of insight for Christian ethics.

We can round out our analysis by pointing out again that no view of revelation or wisdom for Christian ethics is complete unless it incorporates positive elements from all three sources. Christian ethics begins with a theological stance outlining the basic dimensions of wholeness drawn from Scripture (*primus inter pares* among the sources). It finds illustrative and corrective embodiment of that stance in the community as clarified by community ethical judgment. It finds its embodiment further given flesh in the words and deeds of persons as expressed in personal moral judgments. It is in the complementarity and, at times, competition among these media that Christian ethics finds wisdom.

We conclude with a plea for recognition of the truth that the Christian ethicist is much more massively dependent upon ordinary, non-revelatory sources of knowledge than the received doctrines allow for. At one time the Scriptures and church tradition did supply clergy and faithful fully, not only with fundamental insights but with most of the body of knowledge they possessed. In America that day passed with the settlement of the frontier, but the old theories assuming it still remain. Hence Mencken could argue without too much hyperbole:[54]

> The theory that the clergy belong to the class of educated men, once well supported in fact, . . . has not been true for nearly a century. . . . Nine-tenths of the knowledge that they are stuffed with is bogus, and they have very little grounding in what is really true. Since 'The Origin of Species,' indeed, clergymen have constituted a special class of *un*educated persons. . . .

The special contribution of the old revelatory media is to be preserved. Of these, the Bible especially has the function of feeding inflammatory insights for wholeness into the world. One of these, the motif of promise and fulfillment, is the leading insight for Christian ethics as I see it.[55] But it is only a blueprint until it is bodied forth in worldly deed and wisdom. The Christian ethicist today perhaps should take as his model John Lilburne, the seventeenth-century Leveller leader, who "started his reasoning from God and the creation and drew all his premises from the Scriptures," yet "arrived at the secular republic."[56]

By replacing *sola fide* and *sola scriptura* with "promise and fulfillment" known from Scripture, community, and person, the view of revelation and wisdom offered here serves the end of seeking an ethics of the greater community of the ethically concerned. It points toward Christian ethics for a pluralistic society, an ethics that will give Protestants, Catholics, Jews, and ethically oriented secularists common ground to stand on. Yet "promise and fulfillment" as understood here preserves the possibilities of the distinctive views of man held in the Judaeo-Christian tradition and, within that, Protestant Christianity. It is an ethics of continuity and discontinuity, an ethics aimed at the commonwealth of men, at church unity, and at providing a vehicle for the unique contributions that the Judaeo-Christian tradition can now make to the world.[57]

NOTES

1. Josiah Royce, *The Sources of Religious Insight* (New York: Charles Scribner's Sons, n.d.), pp. 5-6.

2. *Ibid.*, p. 153.

3. *The Meaning of Revelation* (New York: The Macmillan Co., 1962), p. 138.

4. Above, p. 56, where we rejected "safety" in favor of "wholeness" as an accurate description of salvation for our times.

5. *The Noise of Solemn Assemblies: Christian Commitment and the Religious Establishment in America* (New York: Doubleday & Co., 1961), p. 131.

6. Talcott Parsons, "Youth in the Context of American Society," *Daedalus*, Winter, 1962, pp. 107-111.

7. Isaac Asimov, *Adding a Dimension: Seventeen Essays on the History of Science* (New York: Doubleday & Co., 1964), pp. 74-80.

8. *Time and Reality: Studies in Contemporary Fiction* (Chapel Hill: University of North Carolina Press, 1963), p. 43.

9. Above, p. 34.

10. Dietrich Bonhoeffer, *Ethics*, ed. Eberhard Bethge (New York: The Macmillan Co., 1955), p. 57 (emphasis mine). Cf. James M. Gustafson on H. Richard Niebuhr: "Theology, he often said, is reflection on the action and nature of God; ethics is reflection on the response of man to the action and nature of God." Introduction to *The Responsible Self*, p. 40.

11. Philippe Maury, *Politics and Evangelism* (New York: Doubleday & Co., 1959), p. 52.

12. This point is discussed in greater detail in my articles, "Love, Justice, and the Non-violent Movement," *Theology Today*, XVIII (January, 1962), 422-34, and "The Cool-hearted Generation," *Motive*, April, 1961, pp. 8-13.

13. Bonhoeffer, *Ethics*, p. 56.

14. Thielicke argues that Christian ethics can no more ignore the data of recent autonomous anthropology than can biblical study ignore the tools of secular literary and historical criticism. "Just the recent self-understanding of man without God, just the atheistic ethos of this man gives us, in the light of revelation, a deeper insight into human reality and unlocks biblical meanings in a way scarcely possible for earlier generations." *Theologische Ethik*, I, ¶¶121-28, 129.

15. Kyle Haselden, *The Racial Problem in Christian Perspective* (New York: Harper & Brothers, 1959); Gibson Winter, *The New Creation as Metropolis* (New York: The Macmillan Co., 1963).

16. H. Richard Niebuhr, *The Kingdom of God in America* (Hamden, Conn.: Shoe String Press, 1956); Jonathan Edwards, *Some Thoughts Concerning the Present Revival of Religion in New England* in *The Works of President Edwards* (New York: S. Converse, 1830), IV; James Sellers, *The South and Christian Ethics* (New York: Association Press, 1962); Edgar M. Hoover and Raymond Vernon, *Anatomy of a Metropolis* (New York: Doubleday & Co., Anchor Books, 1962), p. 27.

Edwards, in his *Thoughts* . . . is sure that "the latter-day Glory" is destined for America. "God has made as it were two worlds here below, the great habitable continents. . . . This new world is probably now discovered, that the new and most glorious state of God's church on earth might commence there: that God might in it begin a new world in a spiritual respect, when he creates the *new heavens* and *new earth*" (p. 129).

17. Paul Ramsey, *War and the Christian Conscience: How Shall Modern War Be Conducted Justly?* (Durham: Duke University Press, 1961); Sherwin Bailey, *Sexual Ethics: A Christian View* (New York: The Macmillan Co., 1963); Roger Mehl, *Société et Amour: Problèmes Ethiques de la Vie Familiale* (Genève: Editions Labor et Fides, 1961).

18. John C. Bennett, *Christianity and Communism Today* (New York: Association Press, 1960), p. 114. This idea goes back at least to the English Revolution. The revolutionaries "thought they were fighting God's battles," but "the course of the Revolution itself led to the emergence of systematic democratic political theories, for the first time in modern history." Hill, *Puritanism and Revolution*, p. 29. The Levellers, "the most advanced democratic group which had yet appeared on the political stage in Europe, fused Biblical and constitutional theories. All men, as sons of Adam, are by nature free and equal under God, whose law is written in the hearts of all men; also the Saxons exercised national sovereignty, under God, through representative assemblies, until the Norman Conquest." *Ibid.*, p. 75.

19. As is pointed out by John C. Bennett in *Christian Ethics and Social Policy* (New York: Charles Scribner's Sons, 1946), a book that has been of considerable help to me.

20. Much more valuable than theological polemics against the press are careful and informed critiques such as Wilbur L. Schramm's *Responsi-*

bility in Mass Communication (New York: Harper & Brothers, 1957); for further discussion of relations between theology and the mass media see my *The Outsider and the Word of God: A Study in Christian Communication* (New York: Abingdon Press, 1961).

21. The ethicist's dependence upon experts in other fields could be the basis for seeking renewed discussion with such professionals and thus become a form of mission. Gibson Winter suggests that the task of informing religious professionals on technological society should be definitely visualized as a calling of the laity and could be "the form through which the Church's witness in metropolitan society will be realized." *The New Creation as Metropolis,* p. 11.

22. "Ethics helps us to understand ourselves as responsible beings, our world as the place in which the responsible existence of the human community is exercised." James M. Gustafson, in treating the thought of H. Richard Niebuhr, introduction to *The Responsible Self,* p. 18.

23. For a suggestive treatment of the Christian appropriation of creational values, see Roger Mehl, *De l'Autorité des Valeurs* (Paris: Presses Universitaires de France, 1957), pp. 219-48.

24. Fifth Oration, "On the Holy Spirit," *Nicene and Post-Nicene Fathers, Second Series* (Grand Rapids: Wm. B. Eerdmans, 1955), VII, 318-28.

25. *Systematic Theology,* III, p. 294. We might also observe that the Trinitarian context affords not only a principle of incorporating "new wisdom" into Christian-ethical insights, but it also provides, if taken seriously, a more balanced theological stance. Much of contemporary theology, in its Christological passions, has de-emphasized the first person of the Trinity and so minimized the affirmation of natural life that springs from a viable doctrine of creation; and the third person as well, and so found itself without a principle for the continual accession of wisdom concerning human wholeness that comes by way of the human mind-spirit.

26. Edwards, *op. cit.,* pp. 426, 431.

27. *Ibid.,* p. 431.

28. In *The Great Christian Doctrine of Original Sin Defended* (New York: S. Converse, 1829), II, Edwards announces that he will examine "human nature, as existing in . . . an immense diversity of persons and circumstances" to evince the tendency and fact of sin. "The way we come by the idea of any such thing as disposition or *tendency* is by observing what is constant or general in *event*; especially under a great variety of circumstances. . . ." Edwards seeks to make his point, in short, on the basis of "the nature of things, as judged by the common sense of mankind." (pp. 310, 321, 407). But having done so, he immediately turns to Scriptural evidences to confirm what reason and observation had discovered. The influence of Locke's epistemology here is apparent.

29. "Temporal Authority: To What Extent It Should Be Obeyed," *op. cit.,* pp. 128-29.

30. That the laity continue to regard Scripture as a sacred text is evidenced in Lenski's study of religion in Detroit, *The Religious Factor,* pp. 336-38.

31. *The Westminster Shorter Catechism* (Philadelphia: Board of Christian Education of the Presbyterian Church in the U.S.A., 1936), pp. 7, 8, 22. The second quotation is from a statement of the board of directors of *Christianity Today,* issue of July 17, 1964, p. 3. The Methodist

affirmation is found in *The Methodist Hymnal* (Nashville: Methodist Publishing House, 1932), p. 512.

32. *The Westminster Shorter Catechism,* p. 36.

33. *Das Geschenck der Freiheit: Grundlegung Evangelischer Ethik* (Zollikon-Zürich: Evangelischer Verlag, 1953). *Theologische Studien,* p. 39. Translated into English as "The Gift of Freedom," in Karl Barth, *The Humanity of God* (Richmond: John Knox Press, 1960).

34. *Das Geschenck der Freiheit,* pp. 18, 22-23.

35. A similar view is expressed by Anders Nygren in *The Gospel of God,* tr. L. J. Trinterud (Philadelphia: Westminster Press, 1951).

36. Emil Brunner, *Christianity and Civilization* (London: Nisbet & Co., 1948), I, 140.

37. Albert Peel, "The Bible and the People: Protestant Views of the Authority of the Bible," in *The Interpretation of the Bible,* ed. C. W. Dugmore (London: Society for Promoting Christian Knowledge, 1944), p. 59.

38. Seward Hiltner, *Sex Ethics and the Kinsey Reports* (New York: Association Press, 1953), p. 48.

39. Cf. John E. Smith on Dewey: "An intelligent being does not merely *react* to the environment, but he is capable of *responding* to it; mind is the response to the doubtful as such." *Reason and God* (New Haven: Yale University Press, 1961), p. 101. Smith offers important criticisms of Dewey, useful in any theological appraisal of pragmatism, although his criticisms are in part answered by Richard J. Bernstein in "Dewey's Naturalism," *Review of Metaphysics,* XIII (December, 1959), 340-53.

40. John Dewey, *Human Nature and Conduct: An Introduction to Social Psychology* (New York: Henry Holt and Co., 1922), pp. 223-26, 232, 274-75.

41. Stuart Hampshire, *Thought and Action* (London: Chatto and Windus, 1959), pp. 119, 169, 177.

42. Robert O. Johann, S.J., "The Return to Experience," *The Review of Metaphysics,* XVII (March, 1964), 319-39.

43. Though he is not responsible for the use I have made of it here, Professor M. J. Lunine of Fisk University supplied the idea of historical consensus to me. What I have in mind is not so much the political consensus sought in our decade by President Johnson as the historical emergence of minimal social standards.

44. *God and the Rich Society,* p. 4.

45. Thus we agree with C. H. Dodd, who argued a good many years ago that the old dogmatic view of the Bible "is not only open to attack from the standpoint of science and historical criticism, but if taken seriously it becomes a danger to . . . public morals." *The Authority of the Bible* (New York: Harper & Brothers, 1929), p. 13.

46. The notion of "criterion" as used here is to be given its full ontological force. Jesus Christ, as criterion of wholeness for human actions, is not merely an example. Our actions are not merely measured by his; they *participate* in his as part of the human pilgrimage toward fulfillment.

47. *Church Dogmatics,* III/2, 342.

48. Thomas Hooker, *Redemption: Three Sermons* 1637-1656, intro. Everett A. Emerson (Gainesville, Fla.: Scholars' Facsimiles & Reprints, 1956), pp. 43-44.

49. *Ibid.*, p. 62.

50. *Nine Modern Moralists*, pp. 4-5.

51. Lenski found an orientation toward autonomous behavior to be a part of the religious expectations of certain religious groups in Detroit, particularly Jews and white Protestants. *The Religious Factor*, pp. 222, 255-57.

52. As alleged, for example, in White, *The Organization Man.*

53. Immanuel Kant, *Foundations of the Metaphysics of Morals* and *What Is Enlightenment?*, tr. Lewis White Beck (Indianapolis: Library of Liberal Arts, Bobbs-Merrill Co., 1959), pp. 58, 87, 89.

54. *Minority Report*, pp. 69-70.

55. Jesus could promise us life in the Kingdom of God because its promise was already being fulfilled in him. Faith is tied to the reality of a Jesus in whom God is already fulfilling salvation in history and through whom we know of the promise of fulfillment. Kümmel, *Promise and Fulfillment*, p. 155. I have not ordinarily stated the motif in Kümmel's abstract theological style for the reasons elaborated above, pp. 63–65.

56. Brailsford, *The Levellers and the English Revolution*, p. 120.

57. Some will argue that my open-ended theory of revelation has left no sure way to convict man of sin. But in the first section of this chapter we considered the use of worldly wisdom for "reconnaissance of the ethos in diagnosis of the human plight." This office of worldly wisdom corresponds to Protestant orthodoxy's religious use of the law as a hammer or mirror to drive men to their knees. Before we study the ethos we get a preliminary insight into sin from the biblical picture of man. As we laid it out in our discussion of the stance (above, p. 59), sin is pretense covering action that breaks up the self, communities, dissevers relations with God, man, and nature. It is characteristically a condition not of inability, the term so sworn by in orthodoxy, but of vast ingenuity and dexterity in private and unilateral projects.

Just as with the picture of wholeness, however, our notion of man's sin cannot be seen in a fully revelatory manner simply on the basis of biblical study and theological reflection. Again, we must turn to the ethos for qualifying and illustrative insight. As a matter of fact, the newspapers probably do a better job than most preachers of reminding us daily of the conflicts, breakups, and persistence of enmities among men, i.e., the continuing sinful condition of the human race. In any case, the ethicist is obliged to become a careful student of the ethos to correct and supplement his own theological understanding of sin as well as grace.

To take an example: it is commonly assumed in contemporary theology that sin appears in our society in the form of destructive anxiety: e.g., the anxiety of death, meaninglessness, guilt and condemnation spoken of by Paul Tillich in *The Courage to Be*, pp. 41, 42-53. But a reconnoitering of American society by the ethicist immediately suggests that Tillich has taken what is indeed an upper-bourgeois form of lostness or unwholeness and has read it uncritically as a generic human predicament. Anxiety states afflict executives far more than workmen, a study by Parke, Davis & Co., reports, according to Vance Packard in *The Pyramid Climbers* (New York: McGraw-Hill, 1962), p. 258. This does not prove that the non-professional, less-educated American is somehow better off, but it does question the universal applicability of a stance that assumes destructive anxiety and mean-

inglessness to be the chief dimensions of unwholeness. Among the non-
professional classes, a proper estimate of the promise of wholeness might
take more account, rather, of nutritional deficiency diseases; or even more
pertinently, of the lack of selfhood that may be implied in the absence
of anxiety states.

A related question is whether contextualist ethics, like Tillich's understanding of anxiety, may not be primarily relevant for the professional,
articulate, educated sectors of society more than for other classes. See
the analysis by Seward Hiltner of the Kinsey Reports to the effect that sex
relations for uneducated groups are natural, like a "flood," and are engaged
in without reflection, without much awareness of questions of conscience
and social responsibility. *Sex Ethics and the Kinsey Reports,* pp. 110-111.
We might hypothesize that a great deal of human activity goes on by way
of reflection and decision-making in the educated sector of society that
happens "naturally," without reflection, among the uneducated.

Part Four

THE THIRD LOCUS:

ACTION

XI

ACTION AS A CENTER OF ETHICS

JOHN PRESTON, the Puritan preacher, used to apologize if in his sermons he tarried too long "in the doctrinal part." The end of theology, he argued, was action. (He lived by this code, too: when he died in 1628 at forty-one, it was said that overwork, along with tuberculosis, was the cause.) If action is the end of theology, it is the very heart of ethics. Our quest of insight, our pursuit of reflection, our use of wisdom are aimed at understanding men as human agents. Ethics is the discipline that addresses itself to shaping and testing human activity; Christian ethics perceives this activity in the light of a definite criterion, God's promise for man, but keeps its sights steadily focused on what man *does* with it. The centrality of human act as response to divine promise is captured in H. Richard Niebuhr's notion of ethics as responsibility: We are called upon not so much to remember God's plans for our lives, with idealists, or to obey God's laws, with deontologists, as to *act as free men*: "God is acting in all actions upon you. So respond to all actions upon you as to respond to his action." Men know themselves as part of Christ's community not as inheritors of an accomplished history of salvation, says Gibson Winter, but as partners with Christ "in the constitution of the New Mankind in history." The prophetic fellowship "is man's work."[1]

Here, manifestly, we come to a new dimension of ethics. We have reached the point, in fact, at which ethics, as reflection, begins to give way to or sponsor morality. At the first locus, we were concerned with the description of a stance, a standard of excellence for human affairs. Based upon the distinctive insights of the Judaeo-Christian faith, our approach was to delineate a theological underpinning that holds out, as end of action, the

promise of wholeness. The Gospel, as promise, is funded or fulfilled from the reality of the Cross rather than by raw activism or
naive "Kingdom-building." Yet the Gospel in its very essence is
that message for man that leaps ahead of itself and enlists human
deeds as part of the very telling: we hear the Gospel of wholeness
only as it evokes wholeness-bent actions in us. Yet with the statement of our stance we did not speak more than implicitly of the
anatomy of human response actions. At the locus of stance, the
ethicist unfurls his banner—*faith*, or *benevolence to being*, or
life in the koinonia, or *promise and fulfillment*, but gives out few
details or battle plans.

At locus two, the problem of wisdom, we made some progress.
We moved from a simple and unitary description of the promise
upon which we stand to differentiated descriptions of this promise according to the pursuits and crises and concerns of men. Such
differentiation and concrete focusing of the promise depends
upon our readiness to use worldly wisdom for probing the ethos.
By recasting our stance with the help of worldly wisdom we have
moved a step closer to man in his reality, man in action. Indeed
we have already encountered man in action, in a sense, because
reflection is a form of action; it is action taking stock of itself, just
as action is "mounted reflection," thought going somewhere. But
fitting out our stance with the forms of wisdom does not get us to
the heart of matters; it does not take us to the arena of actual
implementation of the promise, the arena of human agency.

Thus we posit a third locus, of action. It might be well, for the
moment, to prefix the adjective "temporal" for clarity. The idea
that human beings act or take part or get involved in their own
salvation is a biblical commonplace. The conviction that actions
as such (as opposed to passive, "spiritual" actions) implement the
Gospel is crucial for Christianity rightly understood, despite the
de-emphasis of this category in some strands of contemporary
theology.[2] Men find wholeness through the human enterprise,
divinely commissioned and led, and this enterprise includes cre-
ating values in the temporal world, and re-creating others in
human style.[3] We have already suggested in the delineation of
our stance[4] the thrust of our view, which takes human action to

be real, authentic, and effectual, even when it is "natural" or "secular." For human action has its origin in the divine initiative, and it is substantially the expression and reflection of divine action. Now we must unfold this conception in more detail.

1. Action as context of reality.

We have already called upon the pragmatist approach to knowledge, with its stress upon human initiative, as an aid in translation of the biblical picture of man as *imago dei* into contemporary terms. We can now call on the same tradition to remind us that human actions have become in the modern world the stuff of reality itself. As a concise statement of the pragmatist outlook, we may refer to a classic, though somewhat overdrawn, characterization by John Dewey of the modern emergence of human activity as a way of grasping nature.

The ancient world, Dewey tells us, was seen by its scientists and thinkers as closed and fixed. Reality was permanent and unchanging, and change was something irregular that upset order. This world consisted of a limited number of species and forms and these were distinct, separated, ranged in inviolate orders. The earth was at the center of the universe. The stars surrounding it also were fixed. People were viewed as accepting the kind of order represented in the fixity of the stars: they too had their predetermined places; men were fixed in their destinies. Whatever change took place was regarded as the unfolding of a pre-existent nature (as in Aristotle's teleology, for example). Events were "governed" by mysterious "laws," a conception perhaps modeled on ancient feudal society, in which a ruler governs his subjects.[5]

Man got along in this universe essentially by remaining static. He took what nature threw his way. Science was contemplative, its practitioners sitting by and observing passively. Man was in the grip of nature; his good, according to the ancient Greek consensus, was to harmonize himself with this supervening order.

Since Bacon, Dewey continues, science has taken on a wholly new form, marking a drastically revised way of seeing reality.

The new world of science is an open world with indefinite limits and infinitely varied possibilities. It is understandable only in terms of change. The "laws" of modern science are typically concerned with motion and change (as in the differential and integral calculus). There are no fixed forms and ends, no eternally valid ideals to limit the development of man and the universe according to the static, primitive conception of change as "filling out a predetermined form."[6]

In this universe man operates as its transformer and master. Experience does not mean sitting about vegetable-like to observe nature; it is rather man's active, intelligent effort to subdue nature and make it serve his purpose. The old Greek ideal that man's essence is to realize harmony with nature, to fit in with it, has now been turned upside down. The good now is to make nature fit man. The older point of view took things as they are. The new holds that experience is not passive reception, but doing, transforming. Knowledge does not mean contemplation; it means the exercise of ingenuity and dexterity, it means intelligent activity aimed at making changes. Things are what can be done with them; truth is a quality of activity as measured by the needs of human community. And the proper goal of ethics is the active process of transforming the situation to meet these needs.[7]

It is important to point to the defects of Dewey's picture. Ancient world and modern do not represent the clear-cut contrasts that he sketches. The new, dynamic understanding of reality had its roots in the old world. Dewey overlooks the dynamism of the Hebrews with their sense of history and their apprehension of true humanness as zealous, active response to God. He overlooks the proud self-reliance of some strands of Greek thought (Aristotle's great-souled man, for example). Besides, Dewey seems more interested in specific, piecemeal change than in the larger, ultimate concerns that figure into a full appreciation of history. He shuns speculation and metaphysics and thus has no way of asking questions "about aspects of our life and world beyond the reach of what is taken into account by a philosophy directed only to the instrumental control of things."[8] For all his stress on experience, personal experience—"the life of the self"—almost seems missing in Dewey's philosophy, subordinated as it is to biologism and to public, communal experience.[9] Social needs seem to replace religious concerns, and the wisdom bequeathed modern man by the Judaeo-Christian tradition finds little recognition in Dewey's scheme.

We need not subscribe, then, to some features of Dewey's model. Certainly we may not accept his treatment of theological concerns and the Western religious heritage. Nonetheless, it seems beyond argument that Dewey's description of what is taken for real today is both discerning and basically appropriate. Some such massive shifting of the modes of understanding reality has doubtless occurred in the recent history of Western man. And this revolution is thoroughgoing: it has occurred not only at the level of serious scientific thought, but also at the common levels of everyday life. In the Western world, *society itself is built on the conception that human activity is the fundamental reality*. To illustrate my point that this view has filtered down to everyday pursuits and concerns, I submit the case of casual sports. It is a common assumption that Americans are becoming more and more inactive and, indeed, passive, in their approach to sports. But "reconnaissance of the ethos" shows the assumption to be false. In the past twenty years, the number of Americans who take part in participant sports has doubled—and there are several vigorous new ones, such as skin diving, parachute jumping, and hot-rodding. At the same time, many spectator sports—baseball, for example—have found it difficult to hold fans' interest. This trend has been in course for nearly half a century, and perhaps one of the most fitting symbols of it, for our purpose, comes out of the basketball craze that swept the Midwest earlier in this century. In Muncie, Indiana, reports Robert H. Boyle, basketball became virtually a local religion. "The 1890 class motto had been 'Deo Duce'; in 1924 it was 'To the Bearcats.' "[10]

Counterarguments are easy to supply. Americans go less to baseball games because they sit at home and watch television, an allegedly passive experience. Moreover, the boom in participant sport is largely limited to upper middleclass families with incomes of $7,500 or more and disposable leisure time. But both arguments fail, though they have the merit of illustrating the complexity of our subject and incidentally of the usefulness of making sports the starting point of our investigation.

Our point is that activity is the fundamental mode of viewing reality among modern Americans. By activity we do not simply mean physical work, the burning up of energy, although that is certainly a part of the idea. We have often used words like "ingenuity" and "dexterity" to characterize human agency. Those upper-income families that engage in participant sports do so because they are enjoying the fruits of ingenious, dexterous human action—that is where our leisure comes from. And as for those who do not enjoy participant sports, many are at work climbing the ladder to middleclass status precisely for the purpose of gaining leisure and disposable income (along with status). The same line of argument must be applied to the claim that Americans are increasingly passive television viewers. To be sure, a given television watcher may personally deploy himself much of the time in passive style; let us stipulate, for that matter, that he is flabby, indolent, and uncritical. Yet the appearance of passivity here is misleading.

First, our docile viewer is the end product of a chain of remarkable technical activities which have freed this man from the hold of the environment and given him the option of being docile. We could hardly pick a better example than the television set, in fact, to point to the supremacy of human action in the modern world, for it symbolizes that latest surge of technical ability that has become a revolution all its own, the electronic revolution. A hundred years ago if we had wanted to select representative human accomplishments to illustrate the essence of "activity" we would have chosen the steam engine or some other invention aimed at achieving massive work. But a better contemporary example, by far, is found in the electronic devices designed to expand control of the environment at higher orders of organization than ever before. The classic twentieth-century example of man's activity (and the *hubris* that attends it) is not the steam engine, the dynamo, the automobile, or even, despite the sentiments of the existentialist establishment, the Bomb. It is rather automation.

Since World War II automation has engendered a third epochal upheaval in technology. The first came with the development of machines and created the classical factory system of the Industrial Revolution. The development of mass production was the second. Now, automation has added the elements of "automatic control and decision making," turning the factory "from a haphazard collection of machines into a single, integrated unit." Automation "is a technology based on communication and control," and it enormously increases the quality and quantity of production, reduces lead time, lowers the cost of materials, provides skilled jobs while reducing unskilled ones, and improves working conditions (i.e., affords cleaner plants and improved safety records). But automation, contrary to popular stereotypes, does not find its principal service in factories; there is much more of it in offices. It is a "revolution in the theory and practice of handling information,"[11] a further refinement of human control, far more subtle than the mastery of mechanical power, and far more pregnant in its possibilities. It represents the extension of human activity into new dimensions and its very advent intensifies what we mean when we speak of human agency. We may compare the kind of knowledge represented in conventional astronomy, for example, with the vastly increased knowledge achieved by the photographing of the moon by satellite mission. Henceforth, when one speaks of observing nature, the norm becomes the kind of sophisticated, venturesome wresting of data displayed in the moon shot. Thus "activity" and "passivity," it appears, are both relative terms. The revolution in information technique is our current referent for activity and alongside it, even conventional astronomy, as modern as it is, strikes us as being relatively passive.

Let us get back to our uncritical television viewer, however. We are pursuing the point that activity, in the sense now defined, is increasingly the stuff of reality to contemporary Western society. Is not our television viewer, however, a victim rather than beneficiary of this new view? Is he not a helpless pawn in the grip of "vast, mechanical, impersonal forces" which deprive men like him "of real existence as persons"?[12] Even if we grant that he is, we have the embarrassing problem of explaining how other men we could name continue to think and act with initiative in the face of "mass communication." And in any case, our program of salvation for the uncritical, docile television viewer would be founded on the doctrine of human agency, for we would want him to become critical and to exert initiative. The fact is, however, careful studies of the effects of mass media on the opinion process show that these media do not control us very well. They can indeed reinforce views we already hold, but they are particularly unlikely to get us to change our minds on significant questions.[13]

Far from dehumanizing us, the deployment of human initiative in technical activity has enlarged our possibilities. It has no more "saved" us, of course, than it has damned us. And when men do not wisely employ their own personal intitiative, affluence and technology can become a curse. In the twentieth century, technology has brought "a vulgarized press and entertainment industry, a ludicrous patience with the absurdities the motor-car has brought upon us." But it is also the century in which industrial life opens a much greater choice of "possible kinds of work in contrast with the few choices open to men in the past." Man is perhaps at his highest as a city dweller, as the origin of the word "civilization" attests. The evils of our modern cities represent a price we have to pay, but what is the alternative? Gothic cathedrals went with "filth and beastly diseases"; Victorian sanitation went with "tasteless cities, contempt for the lower orders and a vulgar pushing society that was insensitive."[14]

Hence we cannot contrast human activity and the reality of freedom; they go together. If we are to rethink theology and Christian ethics for our own day, we must bring off some kind of coalition with the the technologists. Living space and neighborhood freedom are part of wholeness. Freedom and living space for our slum dwellers will more quickly come from slum clearance than from further theological polemics against the vast dangers of techniques. For those who protest the impossibility of overcoming forces so gigantic and sinister as the inner city, the counsel of the technologist should now replace the despair of the existentialist. "Slums, blight, and low-income concentration have not been eliminated," one team reports, "nor are they going to be in the near future, but they have been diluted and dispersed to some extent, and will become considerably more so."[15]

It requires no large amount of scientific aptitude to see that a new world view is in the making, and has been for some time. It is a world view based upon human activity as the context of reality. Above all, we must attempt to understand human activity in its most refined, salvific forms: the artificial kidney and the computer more accurately depict human initiative than the pile-driver and the bulldozer. The most representative forms of human agency are those by which mankind realizes wholeness—tenderness, community, justice, and health. Human agency that represents these qualities is sacramental, representative of the divine; it is action that is not merely an appropriation but a *proprium* of divine action. If we must still proclaim the Gospel of the Christian faith to commend these qualities in human actions instead of other qualities, that is because "Preaching is the awakening and making explicit of what is already there in the depths of man, not by nature but by grace."[16]

The dullest pages in contemporary Christian ethics books are those which take up the question of calling, vocation, and work. Until recently, very little new had been said on this subject since Luther defended the calling of milkmaid, and a Puritan divine declared: "Whatsoever we stand in neede of is treasured in the earth by the Creator, & to be feched thense by the sweate of or Browes."[17] But the chapter on calling cannot be rewritten until the nature of Christian ethics has been rethought, and the role of temporal activity given a new basis, one far different from the subordinate one assigned it in the Reformation and never really changed to this day.

2. The interconvertibility of stance and action.

Christian ethics is systematically deficient, we can say immediately, if it treats the theological stance without considering the equivalent of the stance in terms of human, temporal action.[18] It is equally deficient if it stresses "action" without theological clarity upon the promise which the action is supposed to be representing, becoming, or delivering.[19] We do not mean by this, of course, that a systematic Christian ethics must give hints for daily living. But we do insist that the formulation of a promise for the life of man is stillborn and null unless it is amenable to translation into the actual phenomena of human agency, which includes not only the responding act of decision (i.e., the laying-hold of God's promise that we call faith), but implementation by means of initiative, ingenuity, and dexterity. If we could still believe that human beings are saved in the same way a pan of dough in the oven becomes a cake—passively—then systematic Christian ethics could pass over the problem of action with little more than a discourse on decision and an existentialist homily upon the freedom of the will. But for the constructive purposes of Christian ethics (as opposed to, say, liturgics or cosmology), no act of God comes to bear in human life except in and through human acts. That, for some reason, is harder for us to accept than the co-equal truth, cheerfully sworn by, that "the Word of God" in Scripture is expressed in human words. When I speak of human acts, I mean not only personal but social and cultural acts. I would argue that God's will was manifest, for example, in Lincoln's emancipation of the slaves, an act that created a judgment upon one solid sector of mankind, the white South; offered some implementation of the promise of wholeness to another, the slave; and enforced or embodied itself in the more or less morally ambiguous medium of a third, the white North. God's will was, however, only brokenly and distortedly manifest in this event as evidenced by the attendant military conflict and by the failure of emancipation itself to put an end to the suffering of the American Negro. But that raises the question of the inadequacy of every finite action fully to represent the divine, which we consider under the fourth locus.[20]

For dogmatic speculation the field of God's actions is much wider than this, including also "acts of nature." I doubt that the cause of ethical reflection is served, however, by metaphysics. Nature is sufficiently conceptualized, for the purposes of ethics, by the methods of science, whereas human action can be conceptualized only by the combined forces of science, the humanities, and theology. Christian ethics has to do not with the understanding of nature in itself, but with human actions, and with nature only as it is the subject of human actions. Let us take a concrete example—the fateful Alaskan earthquake of 1964, which killed some eighty-one persons and wrought fearful damage to property and the state's industry. Are we not leaving out some of the data of Christian ethics if we fail to think of such events as "acts of God"? I am immediately willing to ascribe the quality of mystery to such events as they bear on human fortune, happiness, and misery. For the rest I am content to accept the point of view of the geologist and seismologist about them. God is to be invoked not to explain physical phenomena but to be praised as giver of life and the promise of the human. Christian ethics is to lay out the meaning of God's acts for the renovation of the human condition. It strays from its task and confuses the state of theology when it divorces its thoughts about God from this understanding.

Such events as earthquakes and tragic hotel fires are fraught with political and social implications that will demand the full attention of the ethicist. Catastrophes serve, in addition, as graphic warnings to men that they are not yet whole. If failure of social responsibility causes some of the hotel fires, an even deeper and more terrifying meaning lurks behind the earthquake, for it brutally thrusts upon man the awareness of the estrangement between him and his natural environment. Yet life goes on; realization of wholeness is our hope despite the continuing cleft in the creation, between man and nature. The Christian recognizes God as Creator of both himself and the universe, but when he reflects on the problems of ethics, he affirms God's choice to be represented in human actions, and he leaves the questions of the workings of nature to scientists and metaphysicians.[21]

Human actions, then, as the locus of the divine action, are in effect a medium for expression of our stance, and from the point of view of a systematic Christian ethics, stance and action are interconvertible. This interconvertibility is bidirectional; an ethical system is like an electrical network in that we may conceive it as having a flow which may vary in intensity and sign. When the flow of ethical concern moves from stance to action, we are involved with *implementation;* when we begin with action as primary and move from there back to ask the question of the stance that the action implies, we are concerned with the demonstrative role of action or, briefly, *demonstration.*

(a) IMPLEMENTATION (movement from stance to action). We have already covered one pertinent aspect, the acquisition of clothing for the stance from the fund of human wisdom. But it is also necessary to talk about the direct relation between stance and action, so avoiding any implication that the funding of revelatory insight with wisdom is somehow an intervening link between promise and activity. Wisdom, from our present point of view, is not so much in the chain of command as in the relation of staff work for logistics and intelligence. Wisdom must indeed be consulted, and the truths of revelation must be squared with and shaped by human knowledge, but the stance is most congruently convertible not into theory or knowledge, but into action. Stance and action are more nearly common currency than stance and wisdom. Wisdom is the staff counsel that we need in ethics in going from stance to action (and from action back to seek its stance).

Thus we arrive at this proposition: *the promise offered in the Gospel is brought to reality by human deeds.* We must immediately prevent any blurring of our proposition from two sides, however. On one side we reject the apparently similar claim of Pelagianism. The primal implementation of the promise is the human deed done by God in the Cross: human deed, because Jesus Christ is a man who acts for his fellow men; done by God, because God was in Christ, reconciling the world to himself. Here the Glory of God shone in man; here was the truly "surprising work of God," which needed no human passivity for contrast, but which indeed came to light by way of the autonomous act of the man Jesus. But at this point we reject the apparently similar claim of fideism. The Gospel has its advent in the human deed done by God in the Cross, but continues its way in the human deeds done by God in the body of Christ—not the institutional church or even the Christ-namers, but the company of men, whoever they are, who act for humanity. Hence we are properly concerned in Christian ethics with any and all human actions that implement human wholeness, as measured by the stature of Christ, whether or not they bear an explicit or confessional relation to the work of Christ.

American social ethics has made a complex of contributions to this view of human action as bearer of the divine promise.[22] One is the renewed insistence that the Gospel may find its way into reality through *imperfect* human actions (just as the insights of revelation find their way to expression through fallible human words and thoughts). A second is that the Gospel makes its impact not only in personal and social acts but indispensably in political acts. A third is that the Gospel can make use of the full spectrum of human acts, from violence to tenderness, though qualitatively speaking, the former is to be judged by the latter. A fourth is that the complexion of an act is always influenced by considerations of time and space—or of history and terrain, to use more expressive language.

The writings of Reinhold Niebuhr best illustrate the genius of these American contributions to ethics. Perhaps most of them are well summed up in John C. Bennett's comment: "Anyone who is concerned about justice must ally himself with those movements which have as part of their dynamic the pressure of group interest in those who are at present victims of injustice."[23] We do not suggest that the elements of realism summed up here—a sense of history, for example—have not also been voiced in European ethical thought. We do insist that the American mind has incorporated these elements more integrally into ethical structures. The introduction of generic human acts (as opposed to strictly faith-evoked acts) into the ethical network involves the Gospel in ambiguity, imperfection, incompleteness and guarantees a positive admixture of evil; yet God's promise to man is implemented in no other way than by this resort to the human. If the promise is thus never fully implemented, still the march of history offers evidence to the Anglo-Saxon eye not only of man's continuing need of redemption but of the arrival of it.

(b) DEMONSTRATION (movement from action to stance). Such
fruits of the promise as love cannot, after all, be laid hold of
except in act. Hence, with a peculiarly dynamic sense of fitness,
the Christian faith insists that promise itself is seen and known
only in act. The human acts of Jesus Christ portray the presence
of God and the hope of man beyond any possibilities of words. In
just the same way the excellences and qualities of humanity are
always best established in the act rather than in a blueprint of the
act or a report about an act. To put it another way, since we
cannot be eyewitnesses to most of the acts, our words are best
employed in pointing to acts. Suppose we are considering, for
example, the qualities of humanity exhibited even in the midst of
war. We are on firmest ground to expound this subject not in
terms of theories of behavior but by pointing to concrete deeds
manifesting human excellence. Samuel Eliot Morison quotes a
poignant excerpt from the war diary of the cruiser *Birmingham,*
for example, after air battles off Leyte in October, 1945:[24]

> The wounded even though suffering shock, in many cases prob-
> ably in great pain until the morphine began to take effect, remained
> quiet and fully co-operative with those attempting to render first
> aid. Again and again I was urged by those horribly wounded to
> help others before themselves. There were no outcries, and in
> cases of those with cuts which were not hemorrhaging too badly,
> when told that those who were bleeding more profusely must
> be tended first, agreed cheerfully in every case saying: "O.K. I'm
> all right, don't worry about me."

With this understanding of the role of action we approach the
New Testament concept of witness. One is to point to what is
going on, to point to the primal deed that brought man back to
God and to himself; and one is so to point by acting himself. No
one can speak in the contemporary world about the act of God in
Christ without using the vocabulary of action to do so. We point
to Christ today by pointing to acts that carry out and express the
act for humanity done in him. We can fairly argue, in fact, that
Christian ethics begins with acts of love and justice, and that the
whole theoretical structure of ethics is but a reading-off of the
implications of such acts. Our stance, in this sense, is a way of

registering the meaning of acts, the acts of Jesus Christ and men. Every act implies a stance, and every authentic act is a demonstration of the Gospel.[25]

3. Action as koinonia, a locus of commonness.

Throughout history Christian thinkers have attempted to seat the idea of "commonness" among men at one of the other loci—stance, wisdom, or fulfillment. Commonness at the stance was the approach of the medieval church and the great territorial churches of the Reformation. In these it was assumed that men were brought under the common banner of Christian morals by the prevalence of a given theological starting point (the authority of creed, bishops, and tradition; "right doctrine"; and so on); society, from this point of departure, was to become a single-molded reality.[26]

It is only with the great World Wars of the twentieth century and the birth of virulent pluralism, nationalism, and secular-oriented societies that the fallacy of making common theology the basis of ethical unity has become fully apparent. There is no common theology any more. Nor can we move to locus two, the arena of wisdom and philosophy, to find ethical commonalty. If societies are no longer held together by the binding word of the Church, neither are they held together by the cement of natural law, or accepted morality, or commonly agreed upon rational norms.[27]

The most usual alternative to these overarching visions of commonness—Christian society, universal moral wisdom—has been the notion of the gathered, separated community that retires from the strife of the world and seeks its own compact fellowship in the life of sainthood (i.e., fulfillment, our fourth locus). The sect groups of the Reformation are the classic examples. But this form of commonalty is gone, too, for there can be no viable *koinonia* today that successfully manages a separation from the world.[28]

Koinonia, the gathering of men into commonness under God must take a radically new form in today's pluralistic world. Instead of uniting on theology or universal truths of reason, instead of withdrawing into a sectarian enclave of saints, we may now have to seek out commonness with other men at the point of action. Men may act together, part of the time, in the hope that at least limited common goods may issue: they may join each other in a commonwealth of actions. While I would not suggest that Karl Barth is a proponent of this view of *koinonia,* his answer to a student is instructive:[29]

> Non-Christians are under the government of Jesus Christ, perhaps against their will and without knowing it. A non-Christian might be applying Christian criteria—and perhaps sooner than Christians. Think of the time of the Enlightenment in Europe or the time of slavery in the United States, or think of the fight for the rights of labor or the rights of women.

Men can at least fight for justice together, Barth seems to suggest, even when they do not share confessional unity. And indeed one of the signal ways in which Protestants, Catholics, and Jews have actually come together in our days has been in common witness against racial discrimination.[30] At the same time, if the three groups attempted to agree on the theological reasons for making the witness, or their understandings of the moral principles involved, there would be conflict instead of *koinonia* (as when the Christians began to state their Christology to the Jews, for example). The same possibility of commonness exists between churchmen and non-believers.[31] We may conclude, then, that the locus of action represents a fresh possibility of *koinonia.* Society can seek its good by coalition and compromise; men can act together for a commonwealth,[32] even when they cannot agree on theology. Each element in the coalition will want to preserve a sense of its identity and know its own distinctive stance: Christians will want to keep pointing out, as their distinctive contribution, the theological basis of humanity and the criterion for quality in humanity that they see in Jesus Christ. But the Jew and humanist must be allowed to present their stances, also. The point at which hands are joined will be common action.

XII

ETHICS AND CONVENTIONAL

THEISM

CONVENTIONAL THEISTIC ETHICS, when it turns from theory to the concrete problems of morality, nearly always builds upon the scheme of a divine-human polarity. On the one hand, there is a *divinely given norm,* usually transcendent in character—called the Will of God, Word of God, or Law of Love. On the other hand, there is the situation of *problematical human conduct.* Since these two entities represent, in orthodox theology, incommensurate realities, the problem arises in relating them. How is the divinely given norm, thought of as a discontinuous absolute, to be accommodated in the human situation? That is the great problem of ethics for conventional theism. Once accommodated, how is this norm to be applied and adhered to? That is its great problem of morality.

In this chapter we will examine briefly some of the ways various recent schools of theistic ethics have solved this problem of getting the norm into the situation. We will be especially concerned with the leading solution of American neo-orthodoxy, which reached representative form some years ago in the so-called "middle axiom" approach. Building on the wisdom that is to be found in these several approaches, we will finally argue that a new model of the ethical problem will be helpful for a reconstructed Christian ethics and that in particular the older approaches that begin with the assumption of a transcendent, absolute norm should be revised. We will go on, in the following chapter, to suggest a new approach based on our promise-and-fulfillment stance.

1. Transcendence and the early Barth.

One possibility within the framework of conventional theism is to view the divine norm as wholly transcendent, operating directly upon society without benefit of mediation through the structures of natural wisdom and morality. The ethics of the early Karl Barth illustrate this approach. "The Gospel proclaims a God utterly distinct from men," says this early Barth. "Salvation comes to them from Him, because they are, as men, incapable of knowing Him." If one asks where the Word of God that guides human conduct is to be found, Barth says enigmatically that it is found in the hearing of it. It cannot be seen incarnated in the conduct of men who have already heard it, for "there is no visible company of saints and exceptional people and heroes." Human righteousness, that is to say, is "in itself an illusion." This word cannot be seen in the frail medium of any human moralities, for Christian ethics does not depend upon human wisdom. The only sufficiently radical word that ethics can speak "is the word which leaping over all so-called intermediate stages, points directly to the mercy of God." Christian ethics means "that there should be no mixing of heaven and earth in the sphere of morals."[33]

The mellower Barth of the *Church Dogmatics* has long since abandoned this kind of lion's roaring (as Barth himself, much later, characterized it). Ethics is a live and increasingly central concern of his theology. His suggestive ethics of "commission" and "exception" makes wide use of varied strands of moral theology and secular wisdom. Yet he still maintains quite stubbornly his older point: just as knowing God in no way depends upon natural theology, but only upon God's speech, so knowing what to do under God in no way depends upon the prompting of natural morality. The Word of God shapes human conduct in and of itself, Barth consistently seems to be saying. It closes the gap between norm and situation by its own thrust into our hearts.[34]

2. Immanence and the Social Gospel.

Though it may be far removed in mood from Barth's approach, the American Social Gospel adopted a solution similar in one way to Barth's. Its God was immanent, found within man's heart and society, rather than transcendent. So there is no vertical "gap" between norm and situation of the sort suggested by a transcendent theism. Nevertheless, the polarity is still there, between the laggard, selfish, heedless society, on the one hand, and the seedlike Kingdom of God within us, on the other. So the problem is still to get the law of love evoked and expanded, but the gap now appears as a temporal one. Men are not *now* living by love, the supreme law of Christ, but since the Kingdom of God is growing among us, they can be expected to change.

In its tender-minded forms, the Social Gospel was just as uninterested in mediating structures between norm and situation as the early Barth. Whereas Barth assumes a kind of self-convincingness about the Word of God, such early prophets of the Social Gospel as Washington Gladden assume a kind of progressive certainty about the unfolding of the Kingdom of God. Gladden tends to exhort men to consult their hearts, just as Barth directed them to seek the Word of God by hearing. Gladden insists straightforwardly that "there is, therefore, more of God in the world today than there ever was before." Men have only to "look and listen that we may see and hear him."[35] This insistence that God is already and increasingly at work among men undercuts the need of a considered theory of social, political action serving the ends of ethics.

It is true that with the tougher-minded Walter Rauschenbusch we do see an awareness of the need for mediating structures of human wisdom to enact in a businesslike way the reforms that will make for social righteousness. But on the whole, Reinhold Niebuhr's appraisal of the movement seems accurate: "It was wrong in the optimism which assumed that the law of love needed only to be stated persuasively to overcome the selfishness of the human heart." It was wrong in its assumption that justice could be established "purely by appeals to the moral ideal and with as little machinery as possible."[36]

The Social Gospel in its softer forms is to be ranked with Barth's *Romans* in its unhelpfulness on the subject of offering concrete guidelines for action. It is simply not true, as often claimed, that in the Social Gospel theological interests were swallowed up by ethical concerns. The theological aspects were indeed de-emphasized, but this lack is not compensated for by the production of reflective ethical guidelines to human action. There is a jump in the Social Gospel from the stance or norm of "the Kingdom of God" to the assumption, largely unargued and unelaborated in ethical theory, of "a progressive reign of love in human affairs." The Social Gospel was concerned with ethical action but not with ethics; there can be no valid Christian ethics, and ultimately no ethical wisdom for practical action, without a theologically conscious approach. The ethics of Barth's *Romans* and the ethics of the Social Gospel in its tender-minded expressions solve the problem of the gap between norm and situation by assuming the self-sufficiency of the norm itself.[37]

3. Natural law and Catholic moral theology.

Unlike the foregoing movements, three approaches deserve attention for their conscious attempts to mediate the gap between divine norm and human conduct. The first is found characteristically among Catholic moralists, who point to natural law (or natural moral law, as it is also called) as a viable medium of the divine word to man. Though "man's call to a supernatural end is certainly beyond the capacities of his nature" (Karl Hörmann) he can travel part of this distance by way of his nature. Man has a subordinate natural end within the supernatural, and the two routes are the same so far as the natural one extends. Man's part journey through the natural, furthermore, is knowable to him by the structures of his own nature, and the nature in which he exists. This structure is the natural moral law, the content of which amounts to "the order set up by God which man must observe in his actions in order to reach his natural end."

This natural law is part of the eternal divine law but it is framed out of the content of human nature. Reason can orient the actions of the self to an ascending scale of ends, beginning with self-preservation and running through self-perfection, care of children, concern for fellow man and perhaps even to "knowledge and worship of the Creator and the ultimate fulfillment of human

existence in union with him," although Hörmann says the last of
these ends "is not recognized by everyone."[38]

Protestants have piled up criticism upon criticism of the use of
natural law as a structure for mediation of the Word of God. I
shall only touch upon some of them here. The oldest, dating from
the Reformation, is that natural knowledge is uncertain because
of original sin. Karl Barth has presented a powerful critique of
natural theology in our time which in effect attacks natural law as
well: God's very nature, Barth argues, is that of a loving, free
Father who characteristically comes to us. The image of our
going to him, even part way, is misleading, and ushers us into the
presence not of the biblical God but of a God-construct. Again,
many Protestants have been influenced by relativistic views of
knowledge, and point out that moral understanding is not the
constant, universal phenomenon that the conventional Catholic
teaching seems to assume; so natural law cannot properly be
taken as a vehicle of common moral norms. Finally, Paul Ramsey
points out that although natural moral law in theory consists of
the deliverances of human reason, which represent part of the
divine order, its content in fact has been frozen for centuries in
Catholicism because of the stamp of official approval that was
placed on earlier understandings of the content of moral law.[39]

Ramsey's point is the most relevant to our discussion. But we
may appropriately shift the ground a bit and direct our criticism
of morality based on natural law not at its knowledge contents,
but at its anthropology. As a guide to ethics, natural-law theory as
it is often conventionally received shares in the ancient estimate
of man cited at the outset of this discussion.[40] This estimate tends
to see man as a passive, contemplative being rather than an
active, initiating demander of knowledge. It leans upon Cicero's
anthropology, with its antique contention that the moral law "is
not a written law, but innate . . . which we are not taught, but for
which we are made; in which we are not instructed, but with
which we are imbued."[41] Down to the very dawn of the modern
era, we can detect elements of this passive understanding of
knowledge in natural-law theory. Pufendorf, for all his dependence on the doctrines of Hobbes, defines law in his celebrated *De*

jure naturae et gentium as "the will of a superior, through which he imposes on those who depend on him action in a manner that he prescribes to them." For Burlamqui, law is to be defined basically as "rule prescribed by the sovereign of a society upon his subjects." Natural law is still seen before Montesquieu, according to his biographer, as "consisting of *a priori*, God-given precepts," or "the fiat of a legislator."[42]

From our point of view, such conceptions of natural law are not to be rejected because reason may deliver sin-distorted knowledge of God, nor because human knowing would seem to usurp God's free speaking, but rather because they seriously underestimate that human initiative in knowing that is at the heart of true wisdom and true virtue.

On the other hand, Catholic natural-law theory, particularly as we learn it from its more subtle interpreters from Aquinas to Jacques Maritain and Karl Rahner, has much to offer. In opposition to some forms of contemporary existentialism the Thomists and Neo-Thomists do insist on the adequacy of reason to reflect on "acts of moral option." The epistemology of Aquinas, Maritain argues, is superior to the arbitrary ethics of modern existentialism, "both because it is rational . . . and because, being founded upon the intuitiveness of the sense and intellect, it associates and identifies being and intelligibility." Such a stance does insist that there is "an order or a disposition which human reason can discover." Fulfillment, on this view, is not the advent of grace at the expense of nature, but the expansion and realization of what is already human. Even in man's natural state, says Karl Rahner, "the beginnings of this fulfilment already exist."[43] Here we receive a powerful clue. Man's active use of reason is already the anticipation of his wholeness. And yet, as criterion of fulfillment, natural-law theory still evokes the aura of conventional theism, with its absolute located in a transcendent realm.

4. The human situation and contextualist ethics.

A second type of mediation offers the human situation itself as the vehicle of ethical guidance. The best examples of situational ethics in the radical sense are the thought of Jean-Paul Sartre and John Dewey. Sartre's existentialism deliberately excludes outer norms and asserts that man finds himself by acting in his situation, by asserting himself. Though Dewey seeks the good of groups rather than the coming to grips with the predicament of the self, his thought in other respects resembles Sartre's. Dewey, too, rules out laws, principles, norms, fixed ends, and the like as models for ethical guidance; morality rather emerges from the active experience of the community as it faces problems. Instead of beginning with principles or ends such ethics begins with the situation and from its crises and encounters and agonies and difficulties derives values, provisional sights ahead, and short-range decisions about what to do next. But all of these inferences from the situation are subject to cancellation by the exigencies of the next situation, for the past cannot bind the present.[44]

Forms of Christian ethics inspired by this approach to morality have come to be called *contextualist* ethics. Instead of beginning with principles and then applying them to situations, "we discover our ethical principles by attending concretely to the situation where persons love, serve, reject, and contend with one another."[45] It is a moot question whether there is any *purely* situational ethics, even in such presentations as Sartre's. Dewey, for example, fully provides for wisdom from the past in his outlook, and he will allow the guidance of a "principle"—if it is validated by experience and usefulness instead of "criteria of sublime origin from beyond everyday experience."[46] The most we can say, then, is that even the professedly normdenying types of ethics at most reject *formal* norms. When we turn to *Christian* ethics, the case is even clearer that there can be no such thing as a purely contextualist version of it. Every ethics tied to the Judaeo-Christian faith assumes an input of past values into the situation.[47]

The usefulness of contextualist ethics lies not in the refusal of norms, as is sometimes claimed, but in its potential of revising norms. First, it may revise the provincial values we bring to the situation, strip them of our illusions. It may add something new in the unfolding of values that was never noticed before. In an early exchange with his brother Reinhold, H. Richard Niebuhr points out that man does not in the Christian setting strive toward ideals, but rather for something emergent from the course of history, "a potentiality in our situation which remains unrealized as long as we try to impose our pattern, our wishes upon the divine creative process."[48] A secondary purpose is to give old values a new chance by seeing them retooled in the developing situation.

Despite the high promise we may be able to discern in contextualism, we should be clear about one thing: it does not give us an escape, as is often claimed for it, from the norm-versus-situation dilemma. The problem of the norm from the outside is rephrased, and contextualism shows us how to make the best of the norm, but the problem remains. In Brunner's ethics there is talk of making decisions according to the situation, but such decisions only give substance to a norm, the divine imperative. Or the norm may be used to specify a certain kind of desirable context, as with Paul Lehmann, who proposes the *koinonia* as model context because this is where maturity in the New Testament sense may be attained. Or the norm may be translated into historical categories as with H. Richard Niebuhr and Gordon Kaufman.[49] But the norm is there; the situation is, in fact, a device for incorporating norms.

5. The "middle axiom" and English-speaking ethicists.

Especially in the English-speaking countries, Christian ethicists have recognized the discontinuity between norm and situation (a point on which contextualism is ambiguous) and sought to bridge it. For this purpose they have been willing to employ the categories of human experience as proximate, provisional media for conveying the ethical imperative. American thinkers seem to have led the way in this endeavor, perhaps because of "the emphasis on religious experience in the movements of evangelical radicalism which have largely formed the American mind and have made of experience a central concept" (Paul Tillich). American theology has excelled not so much at historical study or in dogmatics, but rather in the sphere of social ethics. Continental theology has stressed the difficulties of applying "the absolute principles of the Christian message to concrete political situations." But American Christian ethics has proposed a "rather ingenious" answer: "One found that between the absolute principle of love and the ever-changing concrete situation, middle axioms exist which mediate the two."[50] This is "horizontal" theology, and it has its characteristic American weakness: lack of transcendence and profundity. But it affords a workable solution to the old problem of the gap between the divine norm and the human situation.

The Kingdom of God in its fullness, says John C. Bennett, "lies beyond our best achievements." Yet God does have purposes for us that can be realized. We can define these purposes or goals by the use of "middle axioms," which are "more concrete than a universal ethical principle and less specific than a program that includes legislation and political strategy."[51] Many ethicists point to current conceptions of justice and equality as they operate in race relations as typifying middle axioms. They are theories that have changed with history, partaking concretely of such shifts in civil law as the new understanding that "separate but equal" is inherently unequal. Yet these same changing principles are useful approximations or representations of the more ultimate ethical end of love, i.e., the divine norm. Though this norm may be viewed as highly transcendent in the thought of such American advocates of the middle-axiom approach as Reinhold Niebuhr, this kind of ethicizing is a long way from the Karl Barth of *Romans*. "Barth's view," Niebuhr says, by contrast "makes no provision for discriminating judgments, both because of its strong eschatological emphasis and because of the absence of principles and structures of value."[52]

In one respect, the middle-axiom approach is less satisfying than Barth's early, bold confrontation of the human situation with the nude Word of God. It is an ethics that tends to paper over with its very specialty the current crisis of contemporary theology. It is true that many advocates of the middle-axiom approach, as modern men steeped in historical consciousness, were well aware of the difficulties of beginning with a God or divine norm somehow "out there." And yet the formative writings of Reinhold Niebuhr, to take the most influential figure in the movement, are avowedly dualistic. "Religion in its quintessential character is devotion to the absolute and a yearning after value and truth which transcends the partial, the relative and the historical," Niebuhr urges. A "full-orbed" religion is "dualistic and supernatural in its interpretation." An ethics associated with such a religion will speak of "the absolute in moral terms, love for instance."[53] American neo-orthodoxy has never fully rethought its stance, and is still inclined to define the experience of grace, with Niebuhr, as "the apprehension of the absolute from the perspective of the relative." An unabashed doctrine of transcendence, like that of the early Barth, who sought to build no connecting bridges to eternity, is at least bracing; his *Romans* still hits the *hubris*-clad seminarian like a tubful of cold water. But the middle-axiom approach conceals the gulf between God and man it started with by inserting successively concrete principles.

Still, our argument with the middle-axiom approach is minor. In fact, we do not call for its rejection, but only that it be rephrased consistently in terms of a reconstructed view of experience. On the one hand, lingering references to supernatural absolutes, which indeed do not characterize the movement at its heart, should be expunged. The point of departure should not be in the transcendent, but in an understanding of reality that sees human activity as the standard coin of currency, an understanding which in turn points to a monopolar rather than bipolar picture of the location of "truth," "norms," "values," and so on. There is but one plane of truth and that is the plane in which we shape our lives by initative and agency. But here we must carefully note the implications, as I believe the "God-is-dead" school of theologians mentioned earlier[54] has not.

The problem is not that the divine norm we have been discussing is divine, or that it is a norm, either, for that matter, but that the seat of the divine and the character of the norm have not been redescribed in terms of a contemporary understanding of reality. Modern man still has God and may continue to believe in him. What he can no longer accept is the God-world split as represented in conventional theism. Nor can he accept any view of moral guidance that suggests what he must do to learn is to remain passive. These two features go together: a God above the world who speaks to his dependents. God is known not beyond but within the context of human actions. Man's ethical action comes not in drawing down guidance, successively rendered more available and concrete, from a divine, transcendent norm, but in the active realization of a promise known in a man, Jesus Christ. We no longer can be content with a description of the norm as divine and of the problematic situation as human. Rather, the norm is divine and human at once, for we see real man as *imago dei* in Jesus Christ. And the situation is human and divine at once, for we see men becoming real and reflecting the divine in their actions.

XIII

OPERATING CONCEPTS FOR

FULFILLMENT

OUR FINAL TASK is to sketch in schematic form some of the guidelines for human action compatible with an ethics of promise and fulfillment. Despite the just claim that American Christian ethics is strongest as "social" ethics, there is a small irony here: our pragmatic bent has deterred us from systematic thought in the area of guidelines for action. A respectable start toward a rationale for ethical action has been made in the ethics of the middle axiom, as we have just seen. Now we must profit by the example and reason toward ethical action from our own stance of promise and fulfillment. Calling upon the insights of churchly and worldly wisdom as outlined in our second locus, we can hope to come out with certain concepts of acting appropriate to the realization of wholeness.

To begin with we will do well to heed an early version of the law of parsimony stated by Aristotle for deliberation about human actions. We do not need guidelines for everything. For example, no one pondering conduct deliberates about "eternal things." Nor do we need ethical guidance for actions that are ethically neutral, "things that involve movement but always happen in the same way." We need not even deliberate about the whole of human affairs, not all at once; no Spartan, for example, "deliberates about the best constitution for Scythians." All such things, he says, are outside the scope of deliberation because they are outside the scope of proximate action. "We deliberate about things that are in our power and can be done; and these are in fact what is left."[55]

Granted that our outlook may be in some ways less provincial than Aristotle's (the best constitution for Koreans or Berliners is a matter of interest to Americans, for example), we can still profit by the principle of economy here. Our guidelines should be aimed at shaping human wholeness, and that alone. Moreover, instead of dealing with "wholeness" as one great abstraction (in the manner of revivalists urging men to be saved), we will do well to break it up into its aspects or dimensions. We could do so in several ways. We could treat the vocations of mankind. Or we could treat the several crises of mankind that fend off wholeness —war, poverty, racial injustice, broken homes, and so on. Or we could treat the dimensions of the *imago dei*—man's relation to God, self, and nature.

Still another approach seems wisest. We can also think of wholeness in terms of concentric circles beginning with the self and moving outward through the more inclusive groups. We choose this approach in order to preserve the principle of transcendence, but to avoid the difficulties of a divine-norm versus human-conduct scheme of transcendence. Rather, in our view, each circle of mankind is transcended not by a discontinuous absolute, but by a neighboring circle.

Thus with the model of concentric circles we have an approach to man in space. He is also a creature in time, however, and he marks the passage of time by activity. So we must think of these circles of mankind, or communities, as moving through time. Again, we have supplied a mode of transcendence, for present actions judge or fulfill those of the past, as do future (and past) actions those of the present.

Only one more decision now needs to be made: How many concentric circles shall we work with? Again, let us listen to Aristotle: as few as possible. It seems to us that the minimum number of concentric circles to use as models is three.

The first circle of wholeness is the world of the *self*, the personal sphere, involving the restoration of the self to open relations with God, man (including oneself), and nature. But this sphere is immediately transcended by a second, the enveloping circle of other men.

The second circle of wholeness is the realm of men in *commu-*

nity, or the social-political realm. Here wholeness consists of restoring a sense of the divine in human affairs; restoring justice, openness, and bodily well-being to divers sectors of mankind; dominating nature without exploiting it.

Transcendence also runs in the opposite direction. Even though the human person is a part of political society, he is "also above political society." There are elements in the self, including "the most important and the most sacred," which transcend the group and which raise the entire man to unique status—"this same 'entire man' who is part of political society by virtue of still another category of things."[56] Person and society are mutually interdependent, then, and form mutually transcendent references.

It is clear that we regard wholeness at these first two levels as something realizable in time and space, according to a monopolar rather than bipolar conception of reality. And yet, we are not prepared to close off our circles at this point: to say there is no circle of reality beyond the circle of human society as we know it now would be to fall into unwholeness, into idolatrous worship of what Jonathan Edwards called a "private system." For even the most generous estimate of the breadth and length of mankind, if it is not qualified by some possibility of judgment and further fulfillment, is simply reading the finite as infinite, and that is unwholeness of the direst sort.

At this point we think of the eschatological references of the New Testament. If they cannot now be taken as witness to an end of all things, and of a coming extraterrestrial realm, all the same they do warn us against reading the texture of monopolar reality too provincially. In all of the current theological discussion of the word *secular,* its literal meaning is rarely raised up for inspection. Secular comes from the Latin *saeculum,* age. The secular is literally that which is concerned with its own age. There is a good secularity and a bad secularism. It is healthy for men to know themselves as finite, living in time, and to be aware of the promise and peril of their own time. It is unhealthy (and unwhole) for men to be obsessed with their own age, forgetting the qualifications put upon us both by past and future: this is a shallow sense of time, corresponding in the temporal dimension to the spatial attitude called provincialism.

As the third circle of wholeness, then, I propose to argue that human wholeness also has a final, *eschatological* dimension. It is a judgment upon the narrow sense of space and the shallow sense of time which ever tempts men living in a reality of space and time. It is a judgment at the boundary of this real spatio-temporal life, a qualifying dimension at the horizon of history, in which what is done here and now is both judged as to its lack of fullness and its promised "restoration," i.e., wholeness beyond the narrow here and shallow now.[57]

In sum, we have now provided a six-aspect breakdown of the reality of wholeness. We see man as needing wholeness in three successively transcendent circles: the personal, the social-political, and the eschatological. And each of these dimensions or circles is to be understood in terms of space and time—man's pilgrimage to wholeness occurs, from one point of view, in space, and our actions are decisively shaped by terrain (a theme carefully treated by such novelists as James Joyce and William Faulkner, but insufficiently attended to by theologians); the pilgrimage occurs as well in time, a changing world, in which ethics "must be understood as ethics of the *kairos*."[58] For purposes of analysis we can then seek "operating concepts" for ethical and moral action based on this anatomy of wholeness—one for each aspect:

1. Space-oriented operating concepts:

(a) PERSONAL action in one's space (or place) corresponds to the traditional ethical doctrine of the vocation or *calling*.

(b) SOCIAL-POLITICAL action in group space, i.e., man in his groups living in places and organized into communal spheres of action, corresponds to the traditional doctrine of the *state*, and more broadly, that of the *orders* of creation and society, of which the state is one.

(c) ESCHATOLOGICALLY, man-in-his-place, according to the Bible, is symbolized as the *Kingdom of God* which is finally to replace the nations.

2. Time-oriented operating concepts:

(a) PERSONAL action across a time line corresponds to the traditional ethical problem of *compromise*, which asks for agreement upon what can be accomplished now, and critically involves the question of what is yet to be done.

(b) SOCIAL-POLITICAL action across a time line, i.e., man in his groups living from age to age, invokes the biblical notion of *kairos*, the time of opportunity, and points to the transformation of society through love, justice, and dexterity.

(c) ESCHATOLOGICALLY, man-in-his-time, according to the Bible, faces the *Day of the Lord*, the criteriological time of times.

We are thus equipped with six operating concepts, most of them familiar as miscellaneous ethical doctrines, but which now stand related to each other and to our stance of promise and fulfillment. They are: calling, state (or orders of creation), and Kingdom of God; compromise, *kairos*, and Day of the Lord. At this point I will record my intention to rename one of them, substituting "commonwealth," for "state," or orders of creation. Without making a detailed analysis of them, we can already discern the characteristic kinds of action for each. At the personal level, man acts through *conscience* and *personal initiative;* these are the modes of finding one's calling and deciding about one's future in the compromises with other men that are daily presented. At the political-social level, man acts through *politics* and *technology;* these are the modes of shaping our surroundings into viable commonwealths and grasping opportunities for fuller realization of them in the *kairoi* of history. At the eschatological level, man acts through *prayer* and *worship;* these are the modes of entering the Kingdom of God and facing the Day of the Lord.

We shall have to be content here with brief presentations, finally, of the salient features or current problems of the first four operating concepts: calling, commonwealth, compromise, and *kairos*, reserving further mention of the eschatological operating concepts for the following part.

Calling.

The idea of the calling, according to Emil Brunner, characterizes the concrete "sphere of action" in which we are set by God: "He Himself places you where you are."[59] Insofar as Brunner points to the affinity between the idea of place and that of calling, he offers a suggestive point of departure. But his conventional theism, which depends on the passive anthropology we have so often criticized, is increasingly inappropriate for a doctrine of calling. The notion that a providential act of God establishes us in our places and sets us to work now needs serious revision. It minimizes the elements of decision and initiative that are our chief personal resources for serving God and fellows. It denigrates the idea of place by suggesting that we are where we are regardless of its features.

We agree, then, that the doctrine of personal calling is aptly symbolized in spatial terms. Christian theology has traditionally been biased in favor of time symbols, as in the classical picture of the soul as a spaceless entity, the very opposite of a body. Here, in fact, is the chief difficulty we feel with the older idea of soul. If soul is "movement in time," asks Karl Barth, how could it be this without having "an inalienable spatial complement"? How could it be temporal "if it had no place"? Body "is the openness of soul," "the capacity in man in virtue of which another can come to him and be for him."[60] Man requires space to be in before he can reach out and touch another even with his heart. He requires body, ground, place if he is to find himself, for finding himself means measuring his humanity against the calls on it that come from around him.[61]

Free men realize their calling when they can choose their own places, however, not when they are fixed in them from above. They need such choice not for hedonistic reasons but that they might situate themselves best to serve as agents of fulfillment. The old idea that one must serve bravely and faithfully wherever he may be stationed has its valuable cautionary aspects but can no longer be regarded as the constitutive aspect of the Protestant doctrine of calling. It is at most a part of the counterpoint. Hence the complementary motifs of *terrain* and *mobility* are crucial ingredients of a doctrine of calling. The first asks us to take into account the varied textures of wholeness, the varied absences of wholeness, and the varied modes of enacting it which depend on locale. Here we encounter a guideline for action of the utmost practicality, as members of the non-violent movement in the South have discovered: Nashville, Tennessee, which has elected a pro-civil rights congressman, is a former Confederate state capital; but it is vastly different terrain from Jackson, Mississippi. Techniques of demonstration and protest that worked well in Montgomery, Alabama, and led to desegregation of the city buses, failed repeatedly in Albany, Georgia.[62] One's conscience is to be governed by what needs to be done on given terrain to further wholeness; one's acts are finally governed, as we shall see when we take up the co-equal temporal question of compromise, by what can be done on given terrain to further wholeness. But terrain, in any case, is a decisive ingredient in our personal deployment of initiative.

We are also reminded, at this point, that calling as service to others is strengthened by a sense of roots. In an urban world we must affirm the importance of cutting our roots. We must be free to move to the places where the challenges lie. Yet we do not need to leave old terrain behind us. The future promises most to men who know and understand and revere the past and the place they have come from. The countervailing motif, *mobility,* offers a distinctively contemporary outlet to human aspirations, as the movement of thousands of Americans in recent times from rural towns to cities attests. Mobility, as much as "sticking it out," and probably more so, is now to be regarded as a proper mode of seeking one's calling.

A second set of complementary motifs is *work* and *leisure,* both of which are necessary outlets for the expression of one's calling. Just as orthodox Protestantism emphasized place, statically understood, over mobility, so it has taken the view that the self is essentially realized in work and only incidentally fulfilled in leisure. That Protestants continue to stress the worth of work over such values as "lots of free time" was indicated in the Detroit study of Lenski, which showed such an orientation to be strong among upper middleclass residents and white Protestants.[63] Again, our point is not to urge rejection of this classical Protestant and Puritan teaching. But we do propose a new setting for the idea of work. *First*, we should accept frankly the fact that some forms of work are degrading and unrewarding drudgery, and cease the pretense, still heard from pulpits, that every kind of work, "under God," so long as it is honorable can be "satisfying" and "rewarding," even "enjoyable." A better approach is to support the enterprise of human ingenuity in such forms as automation, which will not control men but free them by reducing drudgery and animal-like forms of work. Automation, of course, will not solve the problems of pride and selfishness, or in fact do anything at all to save us except to widen our choices of what we shall do with ourselves. *Second*, we should strive to make the ideas of leisure and playfulness parts of the doctrine of the calling. Men serve each other by enjoying each other's presence, and so they become whole in leisure and play as well as in producing. *Third*, we should connect up one's work and leisure with his religious faith more effectively. What is the calling of a Christian? It is "building up the body of Christ" (Ephesians 4:12), or, in our own terms, it is acting for human wholeness according to one's dexterity and conscience. The etymological relation between "calling" and *ekklesia*, the Greek for church, should not be overlooked: the congregation consists of the called-out, which we can properly take to be those called out of one pursuit and called into another, the pursuit of wholeness. The congregation is not that of a geographical parish, in the fullest sense now, but consists of those who authentically pursue the personal calling to act for wholeness. Serving as a leader or member of the called-out can still be done in part in the institutional church, but its most challenging frontiers lie beyond, in the realms of work and leisure.

Contemporary Christian ethics, in an understandable concern to avoid endorsing any form of predatory individualism, has probably neglected the personal sphere. It has chosen to discuss sexual relations, to be sure, as an aspect of the person (here the influence of Buber's I-Thou concept has been decisive). On the other hand, contemporary social ethicists have tended to attack racial injustice by proposing social action addressed to groups.

The thinking here is that injustice is more often unchallenged by men in their group life than in their personal life and that so-called "individualistic" approaches to morality are naive if the evils are wrought by groups. But even on pragmatic grounds, I am not so sure that this strategy, alone, is promising enough to justify our ignoring the personal sphere. Men are most vulnerable to conscience when they are confronted as persons, and least so when they can take shelter under the umbrella of group think-ing.[64] But there is another demand on us beyond this pragmatic one (of getting the problem solved), and that is the demand for personal wholeness. Racial justice should be discussed under the heading of personal ethics as well as social ethics, just so as to point up the need of wholeness of those who discriminate.

In addition, we should remember that the wholeness of the community, though it qualifies and judges the wholeness of per-sons (i.e., stands as the transcendent upon every act in the per-sonal sphere), is also qualified and judged *by* personal wholeness. Community is strong only when it consists of whole selves, per-sons capable of making original contributions to the group. Thus the doctrine of the personal calling, while it reaches its transcend-ent limit in the doctrine of the commonwealth, still remains a viable, interdependent concept, and a complete Christian ethics will cast out guidelines for the "person acting in his place."

Commonwealth.

According to conventional theistic ethics, God has organized the creation into ordered aspects. While he is most definitively related to the creation as its redeemer, he acts as "Creator and Preserver," says Emil Brunner, "even where men do not know Him at all." These orders cover the whole setting or place of life, so to speak, and they include both general biological laws and the specifically human ways in which nature and society are under-stood. The orders keep man from chaos while he is awaiting a better state, redemption. For Brunner, the specifically human orders include marriage, family, civilization, culture, and the state. To live in accordance with them does not redeem anyone; the value of the orders consists only in the fact that they create order. They are "a means by which sinful humanity keeps the final consequences of sin at bay: that is, disorganization and chaos." If men are ultimately on the way to love, in the meanwhile they are held in place by the orders, which operate by law, force, and reason, rather than by faith.[65]

This doctrine has been revised in the hands of other contemporary theologians. Karl Barth objects to the separation of God's attributes as Creator and Redeemer. Further, the notion of settled "orders" which govern creation seems to divorce the world from God's continuing, active command. Barth, then, prefers to speak not of "orders" that now seem to be self-contained, but of God's active, continuous "orderings" of creation. God's work is historical, recurring; he continues to deal with his people. It is not partly frozen in the keeping of sin at bay, and partly futuristic in the coming work of redemption. Rather the nations and the other groupings of creation are the subjects of God's loving, redeeming interest all the while, and their sanctification is implied in their very creation.[66]

Dietrich Bonhoeffer also drops the term "orders" and speaks instead of "mandates." In so doing he stresses more than Brunner the role of Jesus Christ in relating God to world. The mandates, or the tasks before man in his worldly existence, are the channels of realizing Christ. All of human activity is to be seen as opportunity for realizing Christ or participating in the reality that he offers. Bonhoeffer specifically discusses four (or five) such mandates—labor, marriage, government, church, and sometimes culture. "Man is at the same time a labourer, a partner in marriage, and the subject of a government, so that there is an overlapping of the three mandates in man and all three must be fulfilled simultaneously." At the same time, the mandate of the Church impinges on man in all these roles, for "it is the Christian who is at once labourer, partner in marriage, and subject of a government." Bonhoeffer argues against splitting off the various activities and groupings of society into separate, autonomous compartments, for it takes them all, taken together, to represent the reality of man, the total way of abiding by God's will that is the path to participation in Christ.[67]

All of these theories are helpful. The grain of truth in Brunner's view is that creation is both good and unfulfilled; that society knows a kind of proximate, rough fulfillment even in unwholeness, as seen especially in our institutions of order and justice. The grain of truth in Barth's is that a dualistic distinction should not be made between creation and redemption—that man, despite his self-frustration that theology calls the fall, is from the outset the subject of a promised fulfillment. The grain of truth in Bonhoeffer's view is that man himself, in the full range of his worldly activity, participates in his own fulfillment.

On the other hand, a conception of orders as broad as Brunner's is too general and diffuse to offer guidance for ethics. The proper concern of a doctrine of orders is not the laws of biology, but, in focused fashion, *those forms of organization of nature and society that bear proximally upon wholeness.* For our time, it seems to me, there are two such areas that stand out above all others: *technology* as the leading mode of organizing nature, and *politics* as the leading mode of organizing society.[68] Such orders as marriage, labor, and education are obviously indispensable to human society and are thus the proper concern of the ethicist; but to the extent that they bear on the fulfillment of the human promise in society, they are all subdivisions of "politics," in the truest sense of this term.

In the second place, conceptions such as Barth's and Bonhoeffer's tend to be restricted in usefulness on account of their high Christology. We have already noticed the difficulty of stating a conception that would unify men according to a common theological point of departure.[69] When we begin to speak of ways of commending wholeness to society at large, as opposed to the inner circle of Christ-namers, we must face the realities of pluralism. The groups and agencies of society represent a coalition of forces for wholeness, presenting varied versions of what wholeness is and how it may be reached. When Christians are thinking of societal wholeness, they must think in terms of the promising aspects of the rest of society that answer, at least in part, to the Christian vision. We can launch joint actions for limited accessions of wholeness in society, and for this purpose can think of the overall linkage of society in the service of "realizing the promise." From time to time we can even join in action-for-wholeness across the deepest fractures of humanity: the United Nations represents such an attempt, or the U.S.-Soviet test-ban treaty of 1963.

I propose, then, that the old doctrine of "orders" and its Christological rephrasings be further modified in an ethics of promise and fulfillment into a doctrine of the *commonwealth*: the organization of society into various joint ventures aimed at wholeness, into various incipient commonwealths, each of which is surmounted by the transcendent possibility of a wider one. In New England, the Puritan fathers dreamed of a "Holy Commonwealth," in which the binding ties were theological and saintly. For our day, the ties should be whatever unity comes from the notion that men, by acting jointly, can secure certain ingredients of wholeness that they could not secure otherwise. (The experience of the thirteen colonies and their later association in a union illustrates the character of these ties.) Christian ethics would not dominate this commonwealth, but it would offer distinctive insight to it by promulgating its own vision of promise and fulfillment, being careful to speak in common coin rather than in the language of theological dogma. It would constantly engage in survey of the values of creation, commending this one, rejecting that one, offering itself accordingly to coalitions of groups in hopes of realizing the benefits of whatever values were held in common.[70]

Under the notion of the commonwealth, criteria could then be deduced for judging the quality of every contributory sector of it—family, church, schools, industry, labor, state, and so on. Formally stated, the leading question would be: How does this sector contribute to the commonwealth or the proximate promise of wholeness that seems attainable in our society?

We cannot hope for overarching unities in the world just now, perhaps never, and especially not on the basis of theological perspectives, which are among the most controversial insights of man. "As the Creator has made no two faces alike," said Jefferson, "so no two minds, and probably no two creeds." Our aim, like Jefferson's, should be, then, not to bring about a unity of thought or theology, but "sociability into the world of thinkers."[71] In history, the commonwealth will always be a changing, multiple entity, consisting of coalitions willing to cross ideological lines in the interest of those modest goals that must characterize coalition politics. At the working level, the coalitions in which Christians act should be kept reasonably small and compact, to allow some cohesion; but made large enough to reap the benefit of intercommunication among groups. (The coalition of Christians, Jews, and secularists, plus the Federal courts, now seeking racial justice is a prime example of one incipient "commonwealth.")

Society, in short, is thought of in our notion of the emerging commonwealth as made up not of static, divine orders, or groups that "ought" to realize Christ, but rather as an array of groups fractured in the fall into competing spheres of interest. At the same time they are groups that can act across those fracture lines to implement limited common goals. The very act of intercommunicating itself is a partial restoring of wholeness, and the content of the common goals is another (in general, the goals will be either projects of politics, designed to organize society more mutually, or projects of technology, designed to increase outer wholeness or health). Christian ethics will work to organize society according to its own distinctive vision of promise and fulfillment in Christ, but it will seek to do so in the commonwealth by coalition. Meanwhile the Christian hope is for an emergent commonwealth that will at last, and indeed, "realize Christ."

Compromise.

We have looked at the two space-oriented operating concepts: calling, which speaks of the personal sphere, and commonwealth, which speaks of the social-political sphere. Now, in turning to the two time-oriented operating concepts, we return to the personal sphere.

If "no two minds" and "no two creeds" are alike (Jefferson), our doctrine of the personal calling unfolds only part of the personal ethical problem. One must not only find the right place for his service, but he must also live in it across time in the company of other persons. To describe this complementary aspect of the personal sphere, living across time in the company of others, we have chosen the admittedly problematical term, "compromise."

Perhaps we should introduce a hyphen and spell it com-promise. A com-promise is a mutual promise to abide by a decision. It is especially relevant as a description of personal ethical activity along the timeline of Christian pilgrimage, for it indicates both the joint nature of the pilgrimage (personal decision always catches us up in mutuality), and man's perennial position "in the middle" between his promise and his fulfillment. The fulfillment is always coming to the band of pilgrims, but it is never historically completed.

In truth, the word "compromise" has needlessly received a bad press in Christian eithics. If we adopt the view that knows of men as infinitely varied in their personal stances, we can see that no calling can be carried out without the approach of compromise. Bonhoeffer has done us a disservice by criticizing what he calls "compromise," pairing it off with another thing to be avoided, "radicalism." In his terms, to be radical is to see only the ultimate, man wholly accepted by God. Radicality overlooks the timeline of pilgrimage, the fact that men are not yet identical with Christ, but only on the road to realizing his wholeness. The radical denies the reality of the "penultimate," in which all things are not yet realized, and to be radical is to be deceptively pious, to deny divine creation itself.

To compromise, on the other hand, is for Bonhoeffer to prefer the penultimate inordinately, to view the ultimate as something irrelevant, futuristic, not available. Both radicalism and compromise, he says, are wrong. Both are opposed to Christ, who is the living representative of the ultimate entering the penultimate. Christ does not free us of the present, nor does he dualistically oppose the present to the final. As to human reality, Christ "allows it to remain as that which is before the last, as a penultimate which requires to be taken seriously in its own way, and yet not to be taken seriously, a penultimate which has become the outer covering of the ultimate."[72]

I accept this analysis, but not Bonhoeffer's use of words. *To compromise, in an ethics of promise and fulfillment, is to promise mutually to accept the penultimate as provisional and as a forerunner of further fulfillment.*

Compromise in the truest sense takes in the whole timeline of pilgrimage—past, present, and future. Abraham Lincoln's understanding of the Declaration of Independence as it bore on the slavery controversy is a compact example of this point. Lincoln preferred compromise to civil war, but only as long as it offered a living mediation of a past promise into the present and future, i.e., only as long as it implemented the freedom implicit in the Declaration of Independence and assured that it would prevail for all. Lincoln's politics of compromise was in direct opposition not only to all extremists but also to moderates who would do nothing to mediate the promise of freedom. The past promise of freedom is worthless to all unless it continues to free men in the present, he insisted. Thus if the Declaration of Independence does not apply to the Negro, "it does not stop with the Negro. Why may not another say it does not mean some other man?" Lincoln asked Judge Douglas. Lincoln equally ranged his strength against the radicals, who wanted to supplant the present with the ultimate. Though the nation had endured eighty-two years, half slave and half free, events were moving toward implementation of the promise of freedom (at least until the backward step of the Kansas-Nebraska bill). So long as this unfolding can be seen, so long as slavery "was in the course of ultimate extinction," men would do well to march along in support and promise mutually to fulfill the original promise.[73]

Compromise also asks us to subscribe to the just-war doctrine of the minimum use of force to accomplish a given end. Men are to deal with each other on the basis of mutual promises, and only when they fail are sterner measures to be adopted.

Though we have chosen to illustrate the spirit of compromise by citing Lincoln's approach to a national problem, yet our basic contention is that compromise is a method of personal action, a way of pursuing wholeness along the timeline of pilgrimage in company with other men, whose versions of wholeness cannot, in the nature of humanity, coincide. Compromise in the proper sense is a mutual agreement to follow time as it unfolds the promise. As the Puritan divine Richard Sibbes put it, "We should neither out-runne, nor be wanting to Providence."[74] It is, in the purest sense of the word, a personal decision to be staunchly *secular*: to witness to the highest possibilities of the age. The spirit of compromise is appropriate, in this tough-minded sense, to the problems of marital relations, racial relations, integrity in business conduct, and the gamut of personal affairs generally. It means that men must begin to love, even if they are not angels; that they must begin to consider the case of the estranged neighbor, even if they are not resolved to save the whole world; that they must begin to initiate wholeness, even if they are not so whole themselves.

Each of our concentric circles is transcended by a wider. The compact circle of personal witness along the timeline of pilgrimage is qualified and fulfilled by the community circle, and we must now consider *social* man in time.

Kairos.

Kairos is the biblical word for "right time," "time for seizing the opportunity," "time of fulfillment." Just as we pictured the "ethical space" of men in groups as a *commonwealth*, a space of mutuality, so now we picture the "ethical time" of men in groups as *kairos*.

In our discussions of the qualities of human action so far, we have called on images that convey a sense of human initiative. We have often used terms drawn from the physical or mental realm: "dexterity," "ingenuity," and so on. Now it is time to remind ourselves that the criteriological action of all actions is *initiative in the interest of the others*. The opportunity that men may seize from time to time, according to the New Testament, is never opportunism, but rather the opportunity to free and enlarge the humanity of others. If we often use physical symbols of human dexterity, such as adventuresome moon shots, it must be remembered that these symbols are shadows or images of divine things, meant to convey with graphic pictures the kind of boldness and daring that men should use not only in physical dexterity but in seizing the opportunity to advance humanity.

On this basis, it is clear why Paul Tillich characterizes the proper mode of action of a true *kairos* as love: only love brings the opportunity for fulfillment that would constitute a decisive *time*. "Love alone," he says, "can transform itself according to the concrete demands of every individual and social situation without losing its eternity and dignity and unconditional validity."[75] If we must necessarily spend much time working on lesser problems, such as assuring order, or justice, or bread, or dominion over nature, we must never forget that the distinctive, crucial problem for Christian ethics is the problem of love.[76] Love is the final action toward wholeness, the heart of community. We are speaking of man in community now, not merely man as person. We think we can depict person-to-person love, that I-Thou encounter that theologians have so celebrated in this century. But what of love on the scale of men at large in social and political groups? What of men who must spend much of their lives functioning not as persons, but as citizens, as professionals, as members of a public society? How do we speak of the criteriological action of love for social man? How do we visualize the movement along a timeline of pilgrimage for men in groups?

The classic solution for neo-orthodoxy and its American variants has been to insist that in *public* actions, justice is the surrogate of love. "Love may be the motive of social action," Reinhold Niebuhr argues, but "justice must be the instrument of love in a world in which self-interest is bound to defy the canons of love on every level." Or again, as he says elsewhere:[77]

> In the larger problems of human togetherness in a complex civilization the witness of love requires that love of the neighbor be transmuted into justice or that it acquire the instruments of justice—which means a rational calculation of competing interests or conflicting claims.

Although this rationale has won wide acceptance, it has raised two serious problems. First, the entirely valid contention that justice is an approximation of love tends to give way, in practice, to the conclusion that justice is a substitute for love. The second problem grows out of the first: once this elevation of justice has been achieved, it is but a further step to the conclusion that justice is the *only* mode of fulfillment available in the *kairos*, for love as *agape* is relegated to the eschatological future as a socially unattainable ideal. Justice passes from representative of the possible to the only possibility; love passes from impossible *possibility* to *impossible* possibility.[78]

To be sure, our neo-orthodox theologians have battled mightily to hold justice and love together. They have good biblical backing. "The Bible knows nothing, or little, of any conflict between justice and love," says Paul Ramsey.[79] But the societal strains have been enormous, and not all the world's theologians and all the world's divines could put the two ideas together again.

The original understanding in neo-orthodoxy was that justice is "what Christian love does when confronted by two or more neighbors," i.e., in a group, as opposed to purely person-to-person, situation. Love, for example, will at least demand that men be unharmed, treated fairly, fed enough, respected as citizens, and so forth, even in situations where men palpably do not love each other. Under the preaching of the Gospel and the practice of love by concerned men in the situation, the theory went, these provisional approximations of or preparations for love, which took the form of justice, might be transmuted into love. Since in the former theological movement, the Social Gospel, this alternative of enforced justice had not been clearly demanded as the instrument of love, the neo-orthodox sought to redress the balance and talked a good bit about justice.

The net effect of the Christian establishment's insistence on social justice in our time, however, has been to force love to the fringes as an unreal alternative, or else as an individualistic responsibility. Justice and love now, as a Negro minister told me, are often viewed among his people as incompatible. "I have read what imaginative thinkers like Richard Niebuhr and Paul Tillich say about the 'interpenetration' of love and justice," he said, " and I know all about the 'creative role' justice is supposed to play in 'pointing beyond itself' to love. But that's not the way it has turned out on the picket lines. We're out for justice. What the Negro and the Latin American and the Asian want today is justice. Let's talk about love later."[80]

What this means is that the human pilgrimage toward wholeness has been speeded up on its frontiers, but never really consolidated. The advance forces, seeking to clear the way of disorder and injustice, have been increasingly successful: justice, though far from fully realized, has been shown to be a live temporal possibility. But the consolidation of community has never been as easily achieved in our century. The ground is cleared, but little has been built on it. This dilemma, I believe, illustrates the chief problem of Christian social ethics for the coming generation: how to rethink the justice-love relationship so that the march forward is really begun again. We must not only attain increments of justice, but we must press on from there into the *kairoi* of restored community relations; we must see in short, that the highest reality, love, is not unduly deferred, brushed aside, pushed into the remote future.

My own view is that the promise-and-fulfillment complementarity offers a preferable alternative to the love-and-justice model, which has in effect now become a polarity or dualism. The movement from chaos through order and justice to love should be viewed as a continuum in time rather than a polarity. To see the possibilities of community as a spectrum rather than as an either/ or choice opens up all kinds of possibilities along the timeline of pilgrimage, some of which seem excluded when the only alternatives in the minds of acting Christians are justice and love.

We could, for example, restore the Stoic ideal of "friendship" as a third notion between justice and love. This category would present the possibility of open and even warm relationships with companions at large in society with whom we have only public or casual relationships. An ethics of the timeline insists that I have a wider choice in public associations than of dealing with men either justly or else claiming to cleave to them in *agape*. It may be possible for me to bring more than mere justice to bear today, even though I do not manifest toward my community fellows the close, searching selflessness that constitutes *agape*. I suspect this third, middle possibility is missing in contemporary theology largely because friendship was an ancient philosophical virtue, which seemed to blur the distinction between *agape* and a hard heart: *agape* is neither *eros* nor *philia,* and a right Christology seems to suggest we should be satisfied with nothing less than the kind of love displayed on the cross, *agape.* Gibson Winter suggests another reason for the decay of the middle ground of friendship in our society: for rootless industrial man, friendships that we so easily cultivated in agrarian settings have simply become impossible. We move too rapidly to maintain "friendships requiring contact and association."[81]

But a new mode of friendship is possible. Let us call it simply "openness" if friendship seems too Ciceronian and agrarian. But let us be clear on what we have in mind. "Casual warmth" is probably the best descriptive phrase, that spirit of initiating speech, for example, between men who are associated in limited or casual fashion. If we had stressed some such model of partial realization in the troubled days when James Meredith struggled to endure at the University of Mississippi, this young man need not have been the "most segregated man in America." Many acquaintances might have done him more than cold justice without as yet the grace to love him—they might have simply been *open* in a casual yet positive way. "It is one thing, and a very good thing, to be acknowledged as a first-class citizen," says Saunders Redding. "It is another and a better thing to be acknowledged a first-class human being. This is the ultimate civility."[82] Thus justice is not the only approximation or surrogate of love. All kinds of human action, from a minimally grudging justice at one end, through openness, acceptance, fondness, and warmth at the other, may be useful approximations. The minimum obligation of the commonwealth is to provide the opportunity for its members to exist as persons; the maximum achievement of the commonwealth is to provide the opportunity for its members to engage in acts of love. In between, there is a vast ground of expanding possibility. The movement of man along his timeline from promise to fulfillment is a fully secular event in the literal sense, requiring us to take seriously each age, and each time of opportunity, in which we live. It is a pilgrimage that needs expanding technology to achieve the ground floor of its goal, but it will be measured not by its success here so much as by its political success, which means the disposition of the human community, at any given point in its pageant, to promote freedom and intercommunication.

Action is the most significant locus of Christian ethics. There is, to be sure, a pre-existent, pre-actual being in man, an ontological readiness that a doctrine of naked action risks omitting from sight. But the truth of all ethics is that this being-in-promise becomes being-in-fullness only when men *act*, take the initiative that is conferred on them as worldly representatives of the divine. Here we have barely been able to sketch minimal concerns for operational guidance of conduct. More is thus to be said, for *shaping* action is not the only responsibility of Christian ethics. We are also concerned with *testing* action. In the final part we must consider the question of fulfillment, and put human actions under that kind of judgment that the New Testament describes as eschatological.

NOTES

1. Perry Miller, *The New England Mind: The Seventeenth Century* (Boston: Beacon Press, 1939), pp. 48, 374; H. Richard Niebuhr, *The Responsible Self*, p. 42; Winter, *New Creation*, p. 84.

2. In much contemporary German ethical thought, a real place has not been made in systematic Christian ethics even for charitable activity (*Barmherzigkeit*). Emil Brunner, for example, criticizes the ancient concept of virtue as a human possession: "Good, in the radical sense, does not mean 'doing good' but 'being good.' . . . The true being of man can never be indicated by a human quality, but only—as is implied in the expression 'to be in faith'—by the actual state of his relation with God." *The Divine Imperative*, pp. 163-65; cf. Herbert Krimm, "Die Barmherzigheit im System einer Christlichen Ethik," *Zeitschrift für Evangelische Ethik*, VIII (May, 1964), 143-51.

3. This understanding of action corresponds to the ethos-probing use of wisdom suggested in Part Three.

4. Above, pp. 60–65.

5. John Dewey, *Reconstruction in Philosophy* (New York: Mentor Books, 1950), pp. 62-76, 82, and *passim*.

6. *Ibid.*, pp. 49, 52, 67-76, 100-106.

7. *Ibid.*, pp. 101-102, 128, 131-47.

8. John E. Smith, *Reason and God*, pp. 94-95, 107-109, 108. In sharp

contrast with Dewey's picture of the ancient world is that which sees the Greeks of the fifth and fourth centuries B.C. as exemplars for the spirit of modern science. They assumed the intelligibility of the universe. Nothing about it was inherently unknowable. "They accordingly believed also in the power of the human intelligence to know all there was to know about the world, and to guide man's career in it." Emmanuel G. Mesthene, "Learning to Live with Science," *Saturday Review*, July 17, 1965, p. 14. Mesthene here is dependent on Gilbert Murray's theory that a "failure of nerve" at the end of this era brought the eclipse of this spirit of confidence and initiative, and introduced a new dependence on God to do for men what they no longer felt confident to do for themselves.

9. Robert O. Johann, S.J., "The Return to Experience," *loc. cit.* Johann, however, is appreciative of Dewey's view of experience, once it is clear that "The fundamental personalism, . . . of my interpretation (as opposed to his biologism) sets us finally apart."

10. Robert H. Boyle, *Sport: Mirror of American Life* (Boston: Little, Brown, 1963), pp. 41, 45, 48.

11. Walter S. Buckingham, *Automation: Its Impact on Business and People* (New York: Harper & Row, 1961), pp. 5, 43-46, 50, 78.

12. The phrase is D. L. Munby's, whose critique of such claims and views has already been mentioned in note 29, Part II, p. 67.

13. Joseph T. Klapper, *The Effects of Mass Communication* (Glencoe: The Free Press, 1960), pp. 17, 21, 45. In a report on a study of the television audience by Louis Harris, *Saturday Review* suggests that there is an increasingly critical outlook and "growing disenchantment with television" among well-to-do, educated American adults. Current programing trends may thus show a willingness to recruit "a mass audience of less and less education and affluence," *Saturday Review's* communications editor fears. "The Fork in the Road for TV," *Saturday Review*, May 8, 1965, pp. 55-56. For further discussion of the ethical problems presented by the mass media in America, see my previous book, *The Outsider and the Word of God.*

14. Munby, *God and the Rich Society*, pp. 46, 52.

15. Hoover and Vernon, *Anatomy of a Metropolis*, p. 216.

16. Karl Rahner, *Nature and Grace*, p. 32.

17. Perry Miller, *The New England Mind: From Colony to Province* (Boston: Beacon Press, 1953), p. 41.

18. "Basic Christian ethics must itself always be theory oriented toward practice." Paul Ramsey, *Basic Christian Ethics*, xii.

19. Gibson Winter, in a critique of "activism" in American church life, comments that members may be impressed into chores that they would consider drudgery at home, "hours of telephoning, cooking, cleaning, serving, endless correspondence." This drudgery itself may be the key, providing a way of atoning for guilt in what is in effect "a Protestant system of penance." *The Suburban Captivity of the Churches* (New York: Doubleday & Co., 1961), pp. 92, 96. Thus it is not the activities themselves that are wrong, or even the amount of them, but the failure to relate them effectively to the quest for wholeness.

20. Below, p. 180.

21. Karl Barth makes somewhat the same point in his doctrine of creation, holding, for example, that "Holy Scripture tells us a great deal about

the sin of man but does not really say anything at all about sin in any other quarter." *Church Dogmatics*, III/2, 139.

22. Above, pp. 75–78.

23. Niebuhr comments in *Moral Man and Immoral Society*, e.g., "a political policy cannot be intrinsically evil if it can be proved to be an efficacious instrument for the achievement of a morally approved end." (New York: Charles Scribner's Sons, 1960), p. 171; Bennett, *Christian Ethics and Social Policy*, p. 21.

24. Samuel Eliot Morison, *Leyte: June 1944-January 1945* (Boston: Little, Brown, 1958), *History of United States Naval Operations in World War II*, XII, 182.

25. Action also has the value of coming in as an exploder of ideological staleness and falsity. Lincoln's formal ethical stance partook of the common assumptions of his time: "I, as well as Judge Douglas, am in favor of the race to which I belong, having the superior position." He believed only that the Negro had an equal right freely to earn his bread. But by *acting* on this latter conviction, Lincoln set in motion an emancipation movement that finally broke through the myths. The Gospel is forever questioning and condemning ignorance, prejudice, and false doctrines of human wholeness. It is likely to do so by the medium of shattering actions. Lincoln's remark is found in Paul M. Angle, *Created Equal? The Complete Lincoln-Douglas Debates of 1858* (Chicago: University of Chicago Press, 1958), p. 117, and in Basler, *Works*, III, 16.

26. Cf. Ernst Troeltsch, *Protestantism and Progress*, tr. W. Montgomery (Boston: Beacon Press, 1958), p. 52.

27. Munby, *God and the Rich Society*, pp. 5, 116, 131.

28. For a picture of the strains modern society places upon sect groups, see John A. Hostetler, *Amish Society* (Baltimore: Johns Hopkins Press, 1963). But the problem is real for all evangelical churches, as Langdon Gilkey argues in *How the Church Can Minister to the World Without Losing Itself* (New York: Harper & Row, 1964).

29. *Karl Barth's Table Talk*, ed. John D. Godsey (Richmond: John Knox Press, 1963), p. 83.

30. As in the conference on race and religion held in Chicago in 1963, in which all three groups participated.

31. As a member of a discussion group at Vanderbilt University composed of theologians and scientists, I have had a good many delightful arguments with an agnostic pharmacologist. If we based any commonness between us upon our two starting points, we would not even be able to argue. He sees the self as an indescribably complex organization of neuronic functions, all of which are in principle subject to prediction by scientific means. The unpredictability of human acts, he thinks, is not to be laid to the mysteries of the "spirit" or of "faith," but only to the presently mind-defying complexity of this neuronic structure. Hence there is no need to talk about God, faith, grace, and so on. My own views are obviously very different. Yet this scholar and I can form a solid front on a great many concerns—academic freedom, social goals, respect for human dignity—mainly because we possess in common an activity-oriented ethics aimed at implementing such realities.

32. Below, pp. 154–158.

33. *Romans*, pp. 28, 74-75, 428. See also Barth's "The Christian's Place

in Society," *The Word of God and the Word of Man*, tr. Douglas Horton (New York: Harper & Brothers, Harper Torchbooks, 1957), pp. 272-327.

34. "Well roared, lion! . . . I still think that I was right ten times over," he says, in that liberal theology "had not seen the biblical conception of eternity in its fullness." *Church Dogmatics*, II/1, 635. For his view of acting under "commission" from the Word of God, reserving the possibilities of "exceptional cases," see the discussion of killing in *Church Dogmatics*, III/4, pp. 397-470. Barth's ethical concerns continue to expand in Vol. IV of the *Church Dogmatics* on "Reconciliation." See also I/2, section 22, II/2, sections 36-39, III/4, sections 52-56.

35. Gladden, *Present Day Theology* (Columbus, Ohio: McClelland & Co., 1913), p. 13.

36. Reinhold Niebuhr, *An Interpretation of Christian Ethics* (New York: Meridian Books, Living Age Books, 1958), pp. 154-55, 159-60.

37. I have not discussed certain other approaches which, in one way or another, seem to me to refuse the option of providing mediation between divine norm and human situation. (1) John Bennett suggests that Lutheran ethics, when Luther's distinction between Law and Gospel is overstressed, makes for a dualism in which men separate their private lives from their lives in the state. The Gospel as norm for societal concerns, in other words, is minimized. *Christian Ethics and Social Policy*, p. 52. (2) Another way out is to hold that the chasm between divine norm and sinful human situation is unbridgeable, at least for the world at large. Certain sect groups (the Mennonites of the Reformation, for example) assumed pessimistically that the world would always reject the Word of God, and so they retired to "islands of Christian holiness in a sea that will always be the scene of violence and injustice." *Ibid.*, p. 45. Today's Mennonites, we must add, appear to be much more interested than their predecessors in changing the world. (3) The divine norm may be turned into a finished morality from above without reference to the situation. This approach is especially seen in American fundamentalism and its sophisticated successor types. The divine norm is seen as "inscripturated" and as thus providing a fixed rule of life. Christian living requires adherence "to these revealed principles of conduct." The Sermon on the Mount is an "ethical directory" with "propositional significance." C. F. H. Henry, *Christian Personal Ethics* (Grand Rapids, Mich.: Wm. B. Eerdmans Pub. Co., 1957), pp. 301-303, 320, 325, 356-58, 362.

38. Karl Hörmann, *An Introduction to Moral Theology*, tr. Edward Quinn (Westminster, Md.: Newman Press, 1961), pp. 50-51, 56.

39. Barth's critique of natural theology appears in *Church Dogmatics*, II/1, pp. 63–128; Ramsey, *Nine Modern Moralists*, p. 213; also see pp. 209-56.

40. Above, pp. 00-00. Gustav Wingren criticizes today's "theocentric" theology for putting the doctrine of Creation "into a secondary place in relation to the fundamental word concerning the revelation in Christ." The motive, he thinks, is our desire for certainty in knowledge. But the result is to put "man and his knowledge, rather than God and His works, into the centre." The result has been to de-emphasize the substance of creation, including cosmology and anthropology. *Creation and Law*, tr. Ross Mackenzie (Edinburg: Oliver & Boyd, 1961), pp. 11, 16.

41. From Cicero's *Pro Milone*, quoted in Hörmann, p. 53.

42. The views of Pufendorf and Burlamqui are reviewed in Robert Shackleton, *Montesquieu: A Critical Biography* (London: Oxford University Press, 1961), pp. 244-47, 252, 264. Such passive views of man and natural law contrast with Montesquieu's own approach, Shackleton says. Montesquieu does not base natural law on "the fiat of a legislator," but upon a descriptive approach to human agency, which holds not merely that men ought to be free, but that they are in fact free. "What Montesquieu attempts to do . . . by means of his descriptive laws of nature, is systematically to characterize the activities of man in relation to nature. . . . The basis on which this *ius naturale* rests is not the fiat of a legislator but on the nature of the created universe."

43. Jacques Maritain, *Existence and the Existent* (New York: Image Books, Doubleday & Co., 1956), pp. 62, 147; Jacques Maritain, *The Rights of Man and Natural Law* (London: Geoffrey Bles, 1958), p. 35; Karl Rahner, *Nature and Grace*, pp. 35-36.

44. Cf., my comments on Sartre and Dewey in "Five Approaches to the Human Situation," *Theology Today*, XV (January, 1959), 521-30.

45. Daniel Day Williams, *What Present-Day Theologians Are Thinking* (New York: Harper & Brothers, 1959, rev. ed.), pp. 114-15.

46. *Reconstruction in Philosophy*, p. 59.

47. As is readily conceded, of course, by discerning contextualists.

48. H. Richard Niebuhr, "The Only Way into the Kingdom of God," *The Christian Century*, April 6, 1932, p. 447.

49. Brunner, *The Divine Imperative*, pp. 130, 134-35, 139; Lehmann, *Ethics in a Christian Context*, pp. 16-17, 54; Niebuhr, *The Responsible Self*, p. 43; Kaufman, *The Context of Decision* (New York: Abingdon Press, 1961), Ch. 2.

50. Paul Tillich, "The Conquest of Intellectual Provincialism: Europe and America," *Theology of Culture* (New York: Oxford University Press, 1959), pp. 159-76. Other English-speaking theologians, too, have contributed to this approach. The term "middle axiom" comes from the writings of Dr. J. H. Oldham in preparation for the Oxford Conference of 1937. Bennett, *Christian Ethics and Social Policy*, p. 77.

51. Bennett, op. cit.

52. *Essays in Applied Christianity*, ed. D. B. Robertson (New York: Living Age Books, Meridian Books, 1959), p. 187. The remark is more applicable to the early than the later Barth.

53. *Reflections on the End of an Era* (New York: Charles Scribner's Sons, 1934), pp. 183, 184, 197, 281, 283.

54. See discussion above, pp. 8-12.

55. *Nichomachean Ethics*, III. 3. 1112ᵃ, p. 354 in *Introduction to Aristotle*, ed. Richard McKeon (New York: Modern Library, 1947).

56. Maritain, *Rights of Man*, pp. 12-13.

57. A more detailed discussion of eschatological concerns for Christian ethics will be found in Part Five, pp. 236-43. See also Mario Miegge, "L'Oecuménisme est-il un Phénomène Cultural Plutôt que Théologique?" *Christianisme Social*, 72 (March-April, 1964), p. 200: A sociological-historical view of the reality of the Church, says Miegge, also acquires, for believers, an "eschatological perspective" in which the historical reality is judged (*mise en crise*), delivered of its errant past, and urged to "die to itself" so it may become anew the witness of the Kingdom.

58. Tillich, *Morality and Beyond*, p. 89.

59. *The Divine Imperative*, pp. 198-201.

60. *Church Dogmatics*, III/2, pp. 373, 401.

61. Cf. Paul Ramsey: "Faith working through love is concerned only to show what *love* is and to discover the neighbor's needs, not to demonstrate that it itself is faithful." *Basic Christian Ethics*, p. 136.

62. Sellers, "A Fuller Definition of Civil Rights," *loc. cit.*, pp. 225-28.

63. Lenski, *The Religious Factor*, pp. 89-91.

64. Sellers, "A Fuller Definition of Civil Rights," *loc. cit.*, p. 229.

65. *The Divine Imperative*, 220-233.

66. *Church Dogmatics*, III/1, 26-29, III/4, 19-23, 29, 36-45.

67. Bonhoeffer, *Ethics*, pp. 73-77.

68. "We have left the familial and productive eras; we have embarked upon a political phase of Western history." Gibson Winter, *New Creation*, p. 126.

69. Above, p. 133.

70. "Christianity invented no new values, and Christian ethics can be expounded by utilizing the values which belong as common property to the discoveries of human civilization, but it subsumes them under a new perspective, which love gives. . . ." Mehl, *De L'Autorité des Valeurs*, p. 242, from an unpublished translation by James Hand.

71. Boorstin, *The Lost World of Thomas Jefferson*, p. 120.

72. Bonhoeffer, *Ethics*, pp. 84-90.

73. Lincoln at Chicago, July 10, 1858, in Angle, *Created Equal?*, pp. 33, 41.

74. From *The Soules Conflict* (1635), quoted in Hill, *Puritanism and Revolution*, p. 247.

75. *Morality and Beyond*, p. 89. See also Tillich's essay, "Kairos," in *The Protestant Era*, tr. James Luther Adams (Chicago: University of Chicago Press, Phoenix Books, 1957, abridged ed.), pp. 32-51; John Marsh, "Time," in *A Theological Word Book of the Bible*, ed. Alan Richardson (New York: The Macmillan Co., 1951), pp. 258-67.

76. Cf. Aquinas on the soul's use of the body: *Summa Theologica*, I, q. 84, art. 6, pp. 392-95 in *Introduction to St. Thomas Aquinas*, ed. Anton C. Pegis (New York: Modern Library, 1948).

77. *An Interpretation of Christian Ethics*, p. 9; "The Quality of Our Lives," *The Christian Century*, May 18, 1960, p. 572.

78. "Love in the sense in which the New Testament uses the word, is not a human possibility at all, but it is exclusively possible to God." Brunner, *The Divine Imperative*, p. 165.

79. *Basic Christian Ethics*, p. 5.

80. James Baldwin, in a similar mood, says: "I do not know many Negroes who are eager to be 'accepted' by white people, still less to be loved by them; they, the blacks, simply don't wish to be beaten over the head by the whites every instant of our brief passage on this planet." *The Fire Next Time* (New York: The Dial Press, 1963), pp. 35-36.

81. *Love and Conflict: New Patterns in Family Life* (New York: Doubleday & Co., Dolphin Books, 1961), pp. 183-84.

82. Saunders Redding, *On Being Negro in America* (New York: Bantam Books, 1964), p. 83.

Part Five

THE FOURTH LOCUS:

FULFILLMENT

XIV

REALIZATION AS END OF ACTION

IF, AT THE FIRST locus of Christian ethics, we make a declaration of our stance, at the fourth, we take the same elements and reshape them into a question. We ask the question of fulfillment. We attempt to assay the quality of human actions up to the hour of testing: how far have they moved us toward realization of the promise of wholeness offered men, as measured by the humanity of Jesus Christ? It may immediately be seen that a systematic Christian ethics, then, resembles that genre of symphony in which there is a recall, in the last movement, of the theme of the first. We re-introduce the stance, in effect, calling upon it now not only as a promise-that-makes-real, but also as a touchstone by which to measure what is real. To put our intent in theological language, here we ask whether a creation gone awry in the fall has accepted the re-creation offered it in the Gospel; or in ethical language, whether man, created to act, has acted for his own wholeness.

At the first locus, we sought the starting point, the self-transcending promise of the Gospel, a promise that includes in its very substance the power to evoke reality-bent actions in men. We went on to consider how the distinctive insights of the Gospel as to this stance are incarnated in special and ordinary sources of wisdom (the second locus). Then we considered the anatomy of human actions as bearers of the promise toward fulfillment, having taken the human deed done by God in Christ as the primal action for human conduct, with which all genuinely human acts are in *de facto* continuity, and by which they are to be measured.

Now we proceed to ask about the conclusiveness of what is happening, the "coming home" of what is promised, the realiza-

175

tion of wholeness in the things men do. Here we are formally in debt to the pattern of movement among the loci of Barth's *Church Dogmatics*: his final locus, too, is the doctrine of fulfillment, or as he terms it himself, *redemption*, which is joined with the earlier loci of God, creation, and reconciliation. Though Barth shifts about in his various descriptions of what may be expected in this unpublished fourth locus (fifth volume) of his dogmatic system, the direction of his thought is fairly clear. The dominant note is that God consummates what he has promised and becomes man's entire future:[1]

> God is the Redeemer. He who has made man and reconciled man to Himself, encounters him in His Word in order that He may be his entire future, fulfilling and consummating what is promised in His creative and reconciling work. . . . In the doctrine of Redemption we must let the Word of God and God's Son Jesus Christ speak to us as the Word of Him who is not only the absolute origin as Creator but also the absolute end toward which we move. . . . Thus the Word of God as the Word of redemption comprehends man from the standpoint of the eternal, i.e., the completed and already consummated lordship of God.

We shall have to ask what this sort of teaching means to men who see both the divine and the future primarily in terms of a monopolar order of reality. The locus of fulfillment, we may say, puts up the results of human action before the test of the reality promised in the Gospel and known in Israel and Jesus Christ and asks how far man as an agent has come toward this reality, how far he has moved in his being and doing "towards a complete man," "towards a whole man" (Ephesians 4:13, 15, 16). It asks this about man not only in his personal sphere but also in his social-political sphere. In both circles, the personal and the social-political, the test is whether men have acted to exercise responsibility for each other and to restore the ties of communication and commonalty.

Barth's stress on the decisiveness of "the last things" in bringing fulfillment sets the predominant mood of our inquiry. But Bonhoeffer's engaging picture of the realization of wholeness among men this side of eternity[2] reminds us, even at this point, that the question of fulfillment is to be put from both directions. Each direction is represented by a doctrine of Christian orthodoxy. To ask about man's fulfillment from the point of view of eternity is to raise the question of eschatology. To ask about man's fulfillment from the point of view of his movement toward the end is to raise the question of sanctification. The second of these, in fact, has been the subject of much of our discussion in this book so far, for we have treated man from the perspective of his ability to act along a timeline that moves toward wholeness. In this part we strive, for balance, to introduce the decisive test of quality afforded by the eschatological perspective. As in each of the foregoing three parts, our procedure will be to lay out formal dimensions of the locus in the first chapter of this part. In the second chapter we will proceed to a critical examination of the cognate doctrines of orthodox Protestantism, which are, for the locus of fulfillment, *eschatology* and the contrapuntal doctrine of *sanctification*. In the third chapter we will attempt a constructive application of our findings to the ethos of an ageric people. But first we must treat certain formal dimensions of the locus of fulfillment.

1. The eschatological operating concepts.

So far in our analysis, we have been taking mankind, for practical purposes, to exist in two concentric circles: the compact circle of the personal, and the surrounding, supervening circle of the social-political. Each circle has its characteristic modes of action and its corresponding expectations.

In the world of the person, the proximate goal is to find one's "place," his *métier*, the sphere of action in which he can deploy his own conscience, dexterity, and initiative; this is his *calling*. But we noticed, immediately, that the concept of the person in his calling is transcended from two directions—by the future (time) and by the larger sphere of the social-political (space). "To be summoned is to be called out of oneself and beyond oneself."[3] As one sets out along the timeline of pilgrimage to realize his calling he finds himself in the company of other persons; one can move into the future only on the basis of mutual promises and decisions (compromise). One's calling is not only transcended by future demands, but also by "larger space," for his calling goes on in a world of *corporate* calling, a world of social-political action in which the human community seeks its calling: this larger realm we have called the *commonwealth*. In it men through politics and technology seek justice and health. The commonwealth, which is pluralistic and flexible in its constituent groupings, is transcended in time by the advent of *kairoi*, new opportunities to open up life for persons and communities. The commonwealth is transcended in space by its own possibilities of enlargement—that is, the possibilities among men not so much of overarching unity as of fuller intercommunication and understanding. (The United Nations, offering incipient intercommunication among discrete national communities, is an example of such "spatial" transcendence.)

Sooner or later these two series of transcending entities must run to the edge of time and space. Or to put it another way, neither series, as such, can transcend time or space. We speak of compromise and *kairos* as ways of dealing with the temporal future. We speak of calling and commonwealth as ways of dealing with man in his human terrain. Our four operating concepts shape human action as spatio-temporal action—and provide judgment for it only on the assumption that time and space are co-extensive with reality.

We saved for further employment, however, two other operating concepts—one an ultimate symbol of space, the other an ultimate symbol of time—the *Kingdom of God* and the *Day of the Lord*. We posited such further qualifications upon lesser space and lesser time out of the knowledge that man is finite. The fact that his reality occurs, so far as he knows, wholly in time and space should not close our eyes to the fact that he is a creature of limits. He is limited in the very same modes in which he is real. He is real in time, but he has not always lived, and will not always live. His society is real in space, but is also limited in space. More to the point, man is always tempted to postulate *exclusive* reality to the points in space and time that he himself knows—the here and the now. He is tempted to see his own calling and commonwealth as the only favored spaces and to see his own present decisions and opportunities as the only favored times. He is tempted, in short, to be *provincial* and *secularistic*— to live in a narrow corridor of space and a shallow part of time, forgetting other callings and commonwealths, forgetting his dependence on the compromises and *kairoi* of the past, and his hope which should be pinned on those to come. Furthermore, man goes the last mile toward lostness when he *pretends* that his space is not a narrow corridor and his time shallow; here he lapses into that spirit of pretension, arrogance, and self-centeredness that is the heart of sin: it can be thought of as *pride* or it can be thought of as *fracture*, for it is a self-deceptive settling upon the place and present of the self or the visible community to the exclusion of men in other places and times.

Men who are real in time and space are then to be qualified, nonetheless, in three ways:

1. Even when they are open to all the possibilities, their time and space is finite.

2. All too often they are not open to all the possibilities, and they live in a hemmed-in space and a shallow part of time: they are provincial and secularistic.

3. Worse, they *pretend* that their narrowness is universality, and that their blindness to past and future is all-sufficiency.

These conditions are, respectively, (1) finitude, (2) underachievement, and (3) sin. The first is not evil but simple createdness. The second is a condition of vulnerability. The third is fallenness. In the next point of this chapter we will treat these conditions in terms of the *inadequacy* of human acts, following our constant procedure of discussing Christian ethics as a question of action.

Here, we add only that we have reserved the two eschatological operating concepts—Kingdom of God, Day of the Lord—to deal with the human problems of vulnerability (under-achievement) and fallenness. As we shall see, eschatology is not only transcendent *judgment,* but also transcendent *restoration.* It is, in fact, predominantly the latter. But we shall have to postpone our exploration of this point until the second chapter of this part, where we will make contact with the orthodox doctrines of eschatology and sanctification.[4]

2. The inadequacy of every action.

In principle we should discuss at this locus the inadequacy of human wisdom as well as human action. Wisdom furthers our pilgrimage by providing the thought world in which the Gospel lives as it is coming to be realized. But wisdom may confound our pilgrimage, too, because human thought can replace action and so defer the march. Human thought can err, clothe the Gospel in inappropriate conceptions, and so take us off the track. This has happened again and again in Christian history as when, for example, early Christians sought to express the stance of the Gospel in terms of the misleading body-soul distinction of Greek thought. Thought, by riveting the mind on the here and now, too shallowly and narrowly conceived, can bring us into that failure to act and fallenness that we have just spoken of.

Unfortunately, there is no safe remedy. We must take the risk of thinking. An "infallible" Church and an "infallible" Bible lead to misrepresentations of the Gospel as deplorable as that of "fallible" human judgment. If the Gospel is to be free, it must be expressed through a consortium of finite media of wisdom, as we have already seen in Part Two. Because we believe the Protestant heritage has allowed the Gospel to speak for itself more freely than the other leading alternatives (no full exoneration of Protestantism is intended) we have been led to insist upon Holy Scripture as *primus inter pares* among these media of wisdom. But beyond that we leave the "safeguarding" of the Gospel to the interplay of Scripture, community ethical judgment, and personal judgment as they struggle to comprehend human lostness and to restore it to wholeness. Thus we have already made our case for the inadequacies of human thought in Part Two.

Human action, then, becomes the specific phenomenon which we seek to test in this chapter according to its power of representing the divine initiative and so of moving us into wholeness.

Let us remember the context, which is fundamentally one of

the *adequacy* of human actions. In Part Four we have already presented our view that human action is, in fact, the only medium for realization of wholeness—which means we have already affirmed its adequacy, and this on the basis of the conception of man unfolded in the Gospel. Do men want personal wholeness? They will find it only as they use their consciences and dexterity to live with others and seek to fulfill them. Do men want to live in a commonwealth, a sphere of community wholeness? They will do so only as they bend politics and technology to the ends of repairing the fractures between men and between men and nature. Love remains the criteriological action of actions, but it depends radically upon these subordinate actions, both to "destroy what is against love"[5] and to embody itself positively.

Also implicit in our understanding of human actions, however, is that they are finite and capable of non-use and pretentious misuse. In very principle, then, we must begin by saying that though our actions are the only medium of God's deeds among men, they can never represent these divine deeds fully. God's purposes are realized in human activity, we can say, without being revealed in fullness or so completed that the Kingdom of God may be claimed as a temporal sequel to them.

(a) FINITUDE. First, we may notice that human actions are to be judged as inadequate by the pilgrimage character of human life, its deployment in space and its movement through time. *Human actions are judged by surrounding human actions and by further, later human actions.* The criteriological action is the deed done in Christ from the Cross. But this deed sets off a train of deeds in history that carry out and express and make good the body of Christ. Yet our own deeds, as part of this *making good,* are only *part* of it, however concerned and dexterous they may be. And as a rule, moreover, the concern is distorted by *hubris,* over-estimation, and so they do no more than reflect and realize in a fragmentary way the deed of fulfillment. Every deed does have the capability of realizing at least that fragmentary degree of fulfillment, but the temptations of human nature, as we have seen, make us want to worsen even this limited contribution by the pretense of its fullness. Fortunately, surrounding deeds and subsequent deeds (our own and those of others, particularly the latter) have the function critically to point to the finitude of preceding deeds. Thus, for example, the string of political and social developments that brought the work week in the United States down from sixty and more to forty hours in this country was a minute sequence of human political acts pointing toward a fragment more of freedom and openness in human life. Yet each step forward (the advance from a sixty- to a fifty-hour week, for example), however enlightened and progressive it may have appeared at its own moment, was corrected by new deeds, which themselves in turn were also inadequate to any full realization of God's purpose. The whole sequence of acts reducing the work week may be inadequate in a fashion undreamed of by its perpetrators: now we are faced with the deadliness of idle hours in this country, whereas the architects of the shorter work week imagined that men would use their extra time to rest, improve their minds, solidify family ties, i.e., serve the ends of wholeness.

The finitude of human actions becomes a problem in yet another way if we recall our earlier recognition that "no given stance will actually be adequate to the whole Gospel." We have insisted that an adequate theological stance for our day, one that does justice to the biblical message, will stress man's initiative and activity as reflections of the divine image in him. And yet what we had to say against other stances in the Protestant tradition must be said against our own: "The Gospel may speak for a given time and purpose through a certain stance, and through one stance more effectively than another. But it is not to be identified fully and finally with any of them."[6] Without yielding our grand point that the modern world sees reality primarily in the context of action, we can still specify the need of listening, by way of corrective, to those who argue for a countermotif. For the foreseeable future, we must attend to rewriting theology in the lexicon of action. But while we are doing so, we must engage in hearing the claim of ontologically oriented theologians from Thomas Aquinas to Paul Tillich, that "being precedes action."[7] This view asserts that at least some partial, inchoate wholeness may be discerned before action, and between actions—in the very being of man, in other words, before it has been dynamically augmented by reality-invoking action. If we must reject this stance, it at least reminds us what we should mean when we base our own stance upon initiative and action. Action is never entered upon for the sake of action, but for the sake of selfhood, community, and wholeness. Action aims at being. If it is true that being is always in the making, and is never to be seen as finished once for all, it is also true that action is the servant of being. It is also true that a full definition of action will include such modalities as quietness, as well as assertiveness; rest, as well as exertion; listening, as well as speaking; giving, as well as taking. If we must continue our stress upon action as defining human beings, let us insist that we are speaking not about "raw activity," but of action bent on pilgrimage.[8]

(b) UNDER-ACHIEVEMENT. In the parlance of educators, an under-achiever is a student who fails to measure up to his possibilities. It is a suitable term for us to use, to describe a condition somewhere between finitude and sin. Though finite and therefore limited, we are capable of more wholeness than we actually manifest. Though limited in space, we ordinarily draw off even more limited spheres for our callings and commonwealths than we have to. Though limited in time, we ordinarily lag behind more than we have to, deferring decisions and passing up opportunities.

Let us put the issue in terms of initiative rather than "hard work." The problem with ageric man, in general, is not that he is lazy, doesn't get things done, or hates work. The fact is that he more often than not depends for his very identity on working to get things done; he probably ought to work even less, in amount, to realize his wholeness. At the same time, his work is not attended by sufficient *initiative*—that is, the expansion of one's horizons into the surrounding space of other men and into the decisions and opportunities of the future. Relationality, as we have seen, is not just a question of action *upon*, but of response *to*, the other. This should not put us off, however. The Christian faith solidly affirms the responsibility of taking the first step—of displaying initiative. (Again, we see the incongruity of images of the self that stress *dependence*, even dependence on God; to respond to God is to *initiate* among men.) Initiative corresponds to Luther's teaching of the priesthood of all believers, which depends upon the Christ-follower's taking the lead to serve his neighbor, not waiting for the neighbor to break the ice or ask for help, much less for him to do the first favor. So it is with human action—it is primary in human life for this theological reason: We reflect God's unprompted grace by unprompted initiative toward others.

One objection to our conception of the initiative remains. If initiating action is the model for finite creatures, and the remedy for the vulnerable condition of under-achievement, why have we chosen as the criteriological action of actions Jesus on the cross? Is this not the most passive of all actions? The very word "passion" used to describe the happening on the cross comes from the Latin deponent verb *patior, pati, passus sum*—to endure, to suffer, to undergo—a thoroughly *passive*, non-initiatory kind of action. Such words as *patient* and *passive* come from this verb and are involved, as the word "passion" itself was, in the idea of *letting something happen* to oneself. If the cross event is criteriological, is not passivity, also? Must we not condemn, after all, the ageric outlook of modern man?

Karl Barth, appraising the quality of Jesus' act for others, rejects this interpretation. "There is certainly no suggestion of a passive mood or attitude," says Barth of this event. "It is not merely that He suffers Himself to be offered, but He Himself makes the offering, and triumphs in so doing."[9] In the cross, Jesus did undergo suffering and death—but at his initiative and for other men. The cross event, far from coming down to us as a model of passivity, then, reminds us of what passion really is: it is the highest form of initiative, not only expressing the act of decision, but revealing its direction, which is toward God and other men. The act of Jesus on the cross does put a qualifying judgment upon every human act, that our doing and acting is never an end itself but is always addressed to the surrounding men and the coming men (not to mention those in the past who acted for us). It insists that genuine initiative is passionate—intensely committed to renewing the being of men. In this sense every authentic action is a kind of incipient passion story—a passionate doing that freely serves the claims of other men.

(c) FALLENNESS. What men can do is limited. This is not the problem. They do less than what is possible to them, and they do so inevitably. Judged by the initiative of Jesus on the cross, we are all under-achievers. We set our sights too much on our own space and time. Hence we become vulnerable to dropping out of the pilgrimage. Even this is not the core of the problem. Men fall not because they are finite, or even because they do not stretch their vision and initiative, though this latter failure opens them to falling. Men fall when they deceive themselves that their complacency is initiative, when they pretend that their self-attention is serving the others, when they stake out a narrow corridor of space and claim to be living in a commonwealth, when they focus upon a shallow present and claim to be living in the *kairos*.

Theologians under Heidegger's spell point to the preoccupation of the middleclass American with gadgets (*Zeug* [gear] is Heidegger's more expressive term) instead of with ideas or persons. At a family reunion the males will discuss fishing tackle, miles-per-gallon, and epoxy cement; the females will discuss drapes, department stores, and medicines. To repair an attic fan or to cook a new Hungarian dish is the business of an entire afternoon. This concern with the gear of living, is not, however, automatically the expression of fallenness. It is, first of all, under-achievement, unavailability to human ends. It is only the *further* step of identifying preoccupation with gear as a human end that we encounter sin and fallenness. To spend an afternoon debating carburetors and to call it human encounter is fallenness. To make a million dollars is not wrong; to make a million dollars and keep it all is not necessarily wrong, though it renders us vulnerable. But to make a million dollars, keep it all, and *claim* to be a public-spirited citizen is depravity, which is the ingenious use of human ability against the stream under the claim of serving humanity. Both selves and nations, Reinhold Niebuhr points out, sin by *pretense*, by denying their limitations. Dishonesty and self-deception are inevitable concomitants, even ingredients, of sin.[10]

If pretense before our neighbors is fallenness, pretense before

God is the root of fallenness. That provinciality which keeps us from seeing other men is a mild form of godlessness, a failure to apprehend the divine in culture. That secularity which keeps us from hearing the past or moving into the future is a mild form of idolatry, a substitution of the worship of the present for the worship of the God of history.

One objection to our conception of sin is sure to come. We apparently are not condemning the misuse of human actions, but only *pretense* covering such misuse. This seems to leave unscathed the man who does not care to join the pilgrimage toward wholeness, *and makes no secret of it.* We seem to be calling George Babbitt a sinner for serving himself while pretending to be a town "booster," but not a Machiavelli or a Nietzsche, who refuses the option of fellowship and never pretends otherwise. Closer inspection will reveal, however, that under our conception of wholeness, pretense is likewise present in a Nietzsche—the pretense that he has the option of "humanity without the fellow man" (Barth). Nietzsche's pretense is more complex than that of the town booster, but it is still a pretense. The booster type may want it all for himself, though he covers up by cheerful service through the Kiwanis club and church board. Nietzsche did not want a fellow-creature drinking at the same well and said so quite plainly. But to deem oneself able to drink at the well alone is the greatest self-deception of all.

XV

SANCTIFICATION AND

ESCHATOLOGY

OUR AIM, in this chapter, is to give some substance to our two eschatological operating concepts, *Kingdom of God* and *Day of the Lord,* to indicate the testing of human actions on the scale of fulfillment. Our goal is to be able to ask in terms of our promise-and-fulfillment stance how real the promise has become in human actions. But this very project puts us, at once, in touch with two older theological doctrines: sanctification and eschatology.

Sanctification is "the realization or progressive attainment of likeness to God or to God's intention for men."[11] In a sense sanctification is complementary to and limited by eschatology, the teaching about "the last things." The *kairoi,* or times of opportunity, come out of some "decisive 'beginning,'" in which a history is inaugurated, and move toward an "end" in which "the content of the age is rounded off and established in its completeness or fulfillment as something eloquent of the glory of God."[12] Without pretending to a detailed study of either of the classical doctrines, we can ask how they support us in our final project of examining fulfillment. We have to ask about these doctrines from the point of view of a contemporary Christian ethics, moreover, which means that we may expect to modify certain conventional features of each doctrine as the result of reflection.

1. Sanctification and the Kingdom of God.

Sanctification has not been an attractive doctrine to the proponents of neo-orthodoxy, probably for three reasons. First, the traditions in the past that have made much of sanctification have often done so seemingly at the expense of justification, stressing the cruciality of becoming godly in works not only as an epiphenomenon but at times as the very condition of salvation. Second, the content of sanctification has often been taken both by its advocates and its detractors to be a more or less pious intensification of simple moralism. Third, in association with the related idea of "holiness," sanctification has often been taken as implying the idea of separation from that which is unholy, ungodly, unclean. Whatever its faults of insisting on the separation of theology from the behavioral sciences, neo-orthodoxy has not been squeamish about consorting with sinners as such.

Whatever the reasons, the de-emphasis of sanctification as a locus of theology has left us with little ground to stand upon. We have chosen, therefore, to arrive at our idea of wholeness by reasoning backward from salvation, as it were, rather than forward from sanctification. In short, we have talked about human fulfillment up to here by passing over the explicit question of sanctification. Now we must raise it.

To be sanctified or to be made holy means to be made acceptable to God, or godlike in our dispositions and actions. The idea, therefore, is not directly a moral one, but only indirectly so. John Calvin was right: genuine faith entails sanctification, and Christ accepts no one whom he does not at the same time set on the road to becoming like him in act. But we have already had to revise our understanding of faith, or rather the Reformation's, in order to establish a modern equivalent of salvation by faith for ageric man. And we must attempt the same for sanctification.

In our terms, to become "godlike" or to be sanctified is to restore one's openness to the divine, to other men and to nature. It is to recover one's initiative. It is to see further around us than the provincial and the secularistic. It is to be made whole: not to be separated by under-achievement and pretense from other men; it is to attain holiness, then, not in the sense of separation from the profane, but in the sense of *completeness*.[13] What we object to in the classical doctrine of sanctification can now be stated concisely. First, it described a state of being rather than a quality of action, a finished state of attainment rather than a quality of openness and freedom to act. Second, it understood man as the receiver of holiness rather than as the agent of it. Sanctification to us means that men see themselves as acting for wholeness and that they really do enact it; sanctification is indeed the teaching that reminds us that only men can love and do justice, for men are the only divine agents in the world.

Sanctification involves a timeline. On this the classical view and our view agree. John Wesley, a proponent of the classical view, argued that sanctification is a "progressive work, carried on in the soul by slow degrees, from the time of our first turning to God."[14] We agree that it is progressive in the sense of net tendency, though not in the sense of uninterrupted growth, for men struggle from compromise to compromise and from *kairos* to *kairos*. Evolution is not smooth but a pageant of conflict and of unique, discontinuous steps forward imposed upon a substratum of continuity. Sanctification is carried on in the calling and in the commonwealth rather than in the soul. It has gone on from the very day of creation rather than from the time of our first turning to God. And it has gone on, as Wesley himself was quick to point out in another context, not as God determines the fate of passive souls, but by the evoking of human initiative: "Though it is God only changes hearts," says Wesley, "yet He generally doth it by man. It is our part to do all that in us lies, as diligently as if we could change them ourselves, and then to leave the event to Him."[15] The role of Jesus Christ in all of this is primary and unique: He re-offers us what we have already been offered from the first day of creation—wholeness. He and his community are the touchstones of what wholeness is for men and nations. He is the bringer of sanctification and the criterion for it.

It should now be obvious that some such doctrine of sanctification has been accepted in American forms of neo-orthodoxy all along, without being called by name. If justice is an approximation to love, then a just man, in his acts, approximates godlike conduct. If justice is the forerunner of love, then a just man, in his acts, is engaged in the process of becoming more godlike in his conduct. Our justice-love polarity, in short, is a form of the doctrine of sanctification. Thus we are not, after all, proposing the restoration of a lost doctrine to contemporary Christian ethics, but rather calling for recognition of one that is already covertly present.

In the Bible and in favored periods of church history sanctification has been recognized as a description of wholeness for both person and community. A "saint," properly speaking, is not an entity to himself, but a member of a saintly corporation. On the other hand, the group is saintly not in any undifferentiated sense, but only in the degree that it is a new reality growing out of the uniqueness of its several members. Sanctification is real at both levels: selfhood and community. This means men never become saintly by giving up their personal initiative in favor of a group, but only by using their personal initiative for the sake of the group. It means groups never become saintly by simply manifesting cumulative "personal" morality, but only by invoking among its members service to a vision of the good of the whole—the goods of politics and society. Community and selfhood go together, then. They are the twin fruits of sanctification. "In any domain," says Teilhard de Chardin, whether it be the cells of a body, the members of a group, or the elements of a spiritual synthesis, "union differentiates. In every organised whole, the parts perfect themselves and fulfill themselves. . . . The more 'other' they become in conjunction, the more they find themselves as 'self.'[16] The more our callings serve the commonwealth, the more they become unique and satisfying callings. The more our commonwealths communicate with each other the more they become commonwealths of integrity. Thus the vision of one world does not mean that every nation gives up its identity, but that the nations cooperate so each may thrive.

The final expansion of the notion of men in groups is the idea of the *Kingdom of God*. It is the promise of new, theonomous terrain in which men will live unbrokenly in service of God, divided no longer by conflicts and fracture lines. The Kingdom of God—or *Kingship* of God—is the symbol of symbols for sanctification in our sense, for it denotes the restoration of openness and availability in Christ of all men on earth and all groups of men. The Kingdom of God is already under course of coming to exist; it is present germinally in the person of Jesus, and the messianic age is already in its beginning wherever men act in continuity with him. At the same time, its fulfillment is not complete at any place or moment, but a consummation may be looked for at the edge of the human scene. With Jesus, "the kingdom of God, in the eschatological sense, had been inaugurated. The eschatological process thus inaugurated would, however, be consummated in the future by a further decisive manifestation of divine power."[17]

With the advent of Judaeo-Christian faith, we can see, God indeed has begun to rule the world more fully than before: a new vision of what it is to be man springs forth here, representatively in Jesus. We do not know as yet what the possibilities are for man, based on this new vision. What we should expect, however, is that man is on the way to new levels of humanity. We must expect "not a halt in any shape or form, but an ultimate progress coming at its biologically appointed hour; a maturation and a paroxysm leading ever higher into the Improbable from which we have sprung."[18]

Our symbol for this ultimate reach of sanctification is the Kingdom of God. It is not a futuristic symbol, however, but an operating concept to be used in the here and now to test and try human conduct. The vision of the consummated Kingdom of God is a spur toward sanctification, and hence a judgment upon man's under-achievement, his failure to extend his vision to surrounding men and future opportunities.[19]

2. Eschatology and the Day of the Lord.

Sanctification in its eschatological reach becomes the Kingdom of God. The symbol of the Kingdom of God, as we have just seen, is to be used in Christian ethics as a critique of our under-achievement, our provinciality and secularism. But a sterner critique is needed. We need a symbol to serve as critique of our *pretenses*, which are what involve us in sin. To arrive at this symbol, we cross over from the timeline of history along which sanctification moves toward the Kingdom, and think imaginatively from the other direction. Let us speak of eschatology and "the last day."

Christian ethics can already take advantage of a good deal of restatement of eschatology that has gone on within the councils of neo-orthodoxy. Yet, we find, more restatement is needed. Classically, the doctrine of the "last thing" has two points of reference. First, it relates to the fate of the *individual* after death. Traditional discussions of post-temporal destiny, immortality of the soul, heaven and hell as abodes, and so on, have taken place as part of this personal aspect. Second, eschatology was set within a *cosmic* or *universal* frame of reference and referred to "events which have generally been considered to constitute the 'last things' for the universe as a whole—the end of the 'age', a day of judgement, future trial and stress or a period of peace and happiness, the destruction or renewal of the present universe."[20]

Contemporary theology has placed more stress on the personal aspect than the cosmic, and it has done so characteristically by construing "last things" not in the strict temporal sense, but in the logical sense, as "ultimate things," the most demanding things in our (present) existence. The reduction is seen clearly in the thought of Rudolf Bultmann:[21]

> Every moment is the *now* of responsibility, of decision . . . every instant has the possibility of being an eschatological instant and in Christian faith this possibility is realised . . . *the meaning in history lies always in the present*, and when the present is conceived as the eschatological present by Christian faith the meaning in history is realised.

There is a strong note here, reminiscent of Heidegger, of "the end" as the test of our present resoluteness or of the quality of our decisions. Are these decisions free of the dead hand of the past? And do they, taken in a crucially important present, move us forward on the way to a future of openness? The great sickness of secularism is not man's interest in activity or empirics, but rather the very uneschatological pretense that the future may be omitted from our concerns. Though we often think of ageric man as dedicated to progress and hence as future-oriented, under the kind of regimen Bultmann speaks of here, this interest in bourgeois progress is seen to be not really future-oriented at all; it is rather a kind of extension of the preoccupations and pretenses of the present into the future. The simplest example is the rising middleclass couple who want a larger (and incidentally more impressive) home. They work hard, save a little, scrimp on items that don't show, borrow, and commit themselves to payments really a bit beyond the level of comfort. This, in effect, is to mortgage one's future to express one's commitment to present values, and it is, at most, a very short-range view of the future. Bultmann's kind of eschatology reminds ageric man that his present stands under a demand from the "other time." The problem with this kind of eschatology is that it is heavily existentialized and limited to personal confrontation. It has made its way to relevance for some modern men, but at the price of leaving behind the older cosmic or universal framework in which eschatological conceptions were classically framed. Contemporary theology, it must be said, has done very little to rethink this larger aspect of eschatology. Some, like Bultmann, have dropped it in process of demythologizing. Others, like Alan Richardson, continue to espouse it unreworked, which is even worse: "The scene of the final salvation must be beyond earth and beyond history in the world to come, beyond time, decay, and death . . . a realm which utterly transcends our experience."[22]

Some betterment comes from those who insist, with William Manson, that the scene of the eschaton "is, it would seem, the world in which man's life is lived and in which Christ died and rose." The "new heavens" and "new earth" of eschatological vision signify not the destruction or displacement of the cosmos, "but its *renovation*."[23] This is a step forward, one that allows us to think of the last things within the monopolar famework of reality, and to assume that any last things Christianity may have to speak about have to do with some decisive transformation of this one spatio-temporal continuum in which men live.

Even so, the weight of classical eschatology hangs heavy over the head of neo-orthodoxy. Whatever is eschatological, the classical view assumes, is done by God, not through human actions but from beyond them and without reference to them. Eschatology has to do with a divine intervention, with a decisive, final demonstration of the discontinuity between God and man. Paul Althaus, for example, commendably speaks of the realm of eschatology as this world redeemed and renewed. Just as Resurrection means a new spiritual body, so it means also, a new world. The new Lutheran theology, he says, has accepted this point realistically, teaching not the annihilation of this world in the eschaton, but rather its transformation. Yet to be excluded in any conception of this world renewed is the role of human activity in it. The otherness of the Kingdom of God does not mean other-worldly, but a transformation *beyond human prospects*: it can come through no man and in no hour of this world. "It is beyond all possibilities of man, of nature, of history." Cultural and political activity have no meaning for the reality of the new world. The new world is not a transformation of earthly cultural processes. *"Unser Ordnen, Gestalten, Erkennen schafft Gottes ewige Welt nicht"* (Our orders, our forms, our judgments do not construct God's eternal world).[24]

Here is the point at which an ethics of promise and fulfillment parts company with such theology. If we can agree that the ultimate reign of God is a decisive reality, "really present in the world," we cannot agree that its presence on earth will have been secured by the action of God in contradistinction to the action of men. Not even the decisive, final act of God is on any different basis from the acts of God we have already been considering, and these come to us in the form of human agency. Christology itself should be the clue to eschatology: God has already acted decisively in the man Jesus Christ; his final decisive act will also be in this Christ—in other words, via human agency.

Where, then, is the test value of eschatology, if we have insisted (a) that its cosmic references are not superterrestrial but continuous with our universe; (b) that its decisiveness as a final event is not to be expressed in terms of divine activity at the expense of human activity? Our answer is that the test value consists in the *content* of the last things rather than a supernatural form of stating them, or in a last-minute reintroduction of the divine-activity vs. human-passivity principle that we have already resolutely eliminated in principle from Christian ethics. This content of eschatology is twofold: it consists of judgment and restoration. *The doctrine of the last things functions as agency of judgment and restoration with reference to human pretense.*

These, indeed, are conventional aspects of the doctrine.

The biblical symbol of the Day of the Lord speaks, of course, of a decisive intervention of God at the time of times, which would be a day of darkness for Israel in view of her failure to realize obedience (cf. Amos 5:18-20, Isaiah 2:9 ff).[25] For us the symbol condemns and rejects our pretenses, our claims to wholeness that only stand as a facade before our provinciality and secularism. No matter how long the world may endure, men will not have moved their commonwealths out wide enough. They will not have grasped every *kairos*. They will not have realized wholeness, but they will have claimed to. They may have moved toward it, but they will have exaggerated the distance. They will still be absorbed with the gear of living and be calling their absorption "humanness." They will still live alongside great fissures in the human terrain, and they will call it peace. They will still exploit nature, and they will call it conservation. The approach of the Day of the Lord reminds us every day that there are "structural elements of unregenerate society," powers and principalities, loose in our commonwealths, that men face the demonic when they cut themselves off from the reach of time and space and live in a shallow world which they, in spite of everything, pretend is the whole. This world, under such self-deception, attracts us "with a force that is not merely the force of sensual stimulation, but of a *demonic power, absolutized finiteness.*"[26]

But the Day of the Lord was not one-sidedly judgmental in Israel. It also suggested another vital content of eschatology: that God as man's Lord would come at last to restore to him his godlikeness, both in his person and in his commonwealth. Stripped of his pretensions, man can face the Day of the Lord and enter the Kingdom of God. This restoration, as with the accompanying judgment, will come to man in a decisive Point Omega at the end of the epoch. It will come through human actions that will criticize and call in question the whole of our present history. But the same human actions, divinely evoked, will also restore what the age hopes for. Speaking of the possibilities beyond prediction for human evolution at the edge of the plane of history, Teilhard de Chardin asks: "What is the work of human beings if not to establish, in and by means of each one of us, an absolutely original centre in which the universe reflects itself in a unique and inimitable way?"[27] Men will see their pretensions and use their initiative to love: that is the promise of the end of the age—at Point Omega. After that time, a new history will have commenced.

The Day of the Lord and the Kingdom of God: these are the eschatological operating concepts which we would juxtapose with the ordinary spatio-temporal operating concepts—calling, commonwealth, compromise, *kairos*. The point is not to bespeak an other-worldly, post-temporal consummation, or to invoke a decisive intervention of a supposedly suprahuman Yahweh. In our view the divine acts in human deeds: God ever is in Christ. Our point with these doctrines is to speak of the test of fulfillment: both the measurement of our under-achievement by the vision of the Kingdom of God and the stripping away of our pretenses by the vision of the Day of the Lord. But the positive side, also, is part of eschatology. That crisis in human affairs that will climax history as we know it will also bring the emergence of man as *imago dei*; for he will learn fully to love and really become god-like only at the end of the age.

XVI

WHOLENESS FOR AN AGERIC

PEOPLE

"AMERICA IS A HURRICANE," writes the novelist Norman Mailer, "and the only people who do not hear the sound are those fortunate if incredibly stupid and smug White Protestants who live in the center, in the serene eye of the big wind."[28] If America is a hurricane of furious action (the best of it sexual and "hip" from Mailer's point of view), the power structures and the community ethical forces are all too often divorced from it. The very centers in our society that ought to be leading have failed to appear where the action is. Activity, which could bring man wholeness, and ethics, which could lead him to it, are poles apart.

What the Christian, Jewish, and other ethically oriented forces of our world must not fail to realize is this: Ageric man now holds the torch, which has been passed him from the former bearers of history. He has surpassed the highest types of man hitherto known—the learned man of the Renaissance, the believing man of the Reformation, the rational man of the Enlightenment, the romantic man of the nineteenth century. The model man of the Reformation was free because he could believe for himself. The model participant in the Enlightenment was free because he could think for himself. Ageric man, if he were on intimate terms with his own promise, would know he is free because he can act for himself in the double sense of personal and community intiative that we have been discussing. It is the business of Christian ethics to acquaint ageric man with his promise.

Ageric man acts without knowing that action is the basis of his freedom. His activity is raw, undirected, circular, devoted to short excursions into the near-range future, but not pressed into a pilgrimage toward humanity: a pilgrimage that began on the day of creation, found definitive embodiment in Jesus Christ, took on ever new freshness of implementation in the course of human affairs, e.g., the Declaration of Independence, or the expansion in England of the right to own property, from crown to gentry and commoner.

Ageric man is first an under-achiever. We see the raw stuff of humanity in the surging frenzy of the middleclass, which far from being committed to the status quo, channels its drive and energy toward the American peerage of affluence and spare time (spare time, not leisure). Human activity is the divine possibility in human life, but only when it is used to support the human as such; when this divine possibility is used to support a less than human project, we see the results in the frustrations and neuroses of America: in the businessmen visiting the New York World's Fair who could "tear themselves away from their offices but not from the stock tickers" and besieged officials for market news;[29] in the looting and riots of 1964 that swept Harlem and other cities with only the most tenuous relation to the struggle for civil rights; in the morning vodka klatsch of suburban housewives, laid off from the human enterprise.

Ageric man is a frustrated under-achiever because he has the Puritan drive without the Puritan eschatology. The Puritans, too, never found full wholeness; their Holy Commonwealth foundered after a generation or two. The Puritans did find finite wholeness by positing sainthood as the concomitant and really the reward of trade: they were the most successful trader-saints in history, and their theologians, from Perkins and Preston in England down to Stoddard and Edwards in Northampton, Massachusetts, gave them a theological basis for their commercial preoccupations. Perhaps it is the heritage of this synthetic theology, which aimed ageric energy at sainthood, that has saved modern ageric man in America from an even worse fate than the neurosis of middleclass under-achievement: in other situations, modern man when released both from the burden of excessive labor and from supernatural heteronomy has plunged further. He fell a ready victim to Hitler, for example, who knew how to corral this excess energy of the modern bourgeoisie, an energy geometrically increased by technical productivity, and knew how to release it within the closed system of Nazism. In America this excess energy has been channeled into less destructive ends, and typically, leadership has been exerted more by movie stars and improbable singers than by political tyrants. The under-achievement of American ageric man is typified in his provinciality and secularism, in his commitment to short-run goals, in his weakness for the equipment of living—appliances and automobiles.

But ageric man is not merely an under-achiever. He is also a pretender, a self-deceiver, who claims to be realizing the human with his possibilities. In America the common man is more or less afflicted by what Richard Hofstadter calls "the one-hundred percent mentality." It is a kind of self-righteousness stemming from our conservative religious past, mixed with "fundamentalist Americanism." The one-hundred percenter "will tolerate no ambiguities, no equivocations, no reservations, and no criticism."[30] It is his stolid insistence on his own wholeness that finally carries him away into lostness. Because his actions are never wholly without reference to humanity his lostness is not that either/or damnation of orthodoxy. It is rather the lostness of lagging behind and being closed off from the best possibilities. It is the lostness of never being quite satisfied, of always needing a bit more of something. It is the lostness of dexterous activity that is, at best, not quite good enough. But it is most of all the lostness of taking oneself out of action, for that is the direct result of the pretense to wholeness: we lose our initiative toward calling and commonwealth. The one-hundred percenter will not compromise, will not risk a joint venture with another commonwealth as a means of seizing opportunity. Since the pilgrimage cannot be stayed, it is the others, on their calling, and the commonwealth itself, who move ahead and leave him behind.

The task of the Christian ethicist is to restore human activity so that it reflects the glory of God. This means restoring it to the service of the promise of the Gospel. It means, in spatio-temporal terms, restoring it to a place in the struggle to be human.

The under-achievement of ageric man is to be amended by

reintroducing the aim of human initiative. This aim is neither other-worldly existence, nor fixing the attic fan. It is rather the breaking down of barriers between men and the subordinate healing of wounds from the struggle with nature.

Since the Kingdom of God is pressing in upon us, but is not yet here, this restoring of barriers must not be presented in utopian terms, which is standard operating procedure for neo-orthodoxy. At the present stage of our pilgrimage, the goal of wholeness may generally be described better as *intercommunication* than as seamless union. Our society is pluralistic rather than monolithic, and the ends of calling and community will be served for some time to come by restoring coalitions and communication than by structural merger. Despite the new spirit of cooperation among our religious faiths, for example, Lenski found evidence in Detroit that the sense of identity among socio-religious groups is growing, rather than receding.[31] If he is right, this development has great implications for our model of commonwealth, and it means our efforts should be directed toward the reduction of tensions and the ferreting out of common goals. Indeed, striving for balance and varied contributions from competing sectors of society may be what is most healthy. Such students as D. L. Munby are in fact bitingly critical of "the usual run of Christian anodynes," particularly those associated with the ecumenical movement, that assume wholeness means a common morality or theology. "We cannot assume any common religious scale of values," he says. "The facts are too diverse, society is too complex, and the human mind is too limited." Moreover, it may be the Christian's duty, from time to time, to take sides rather than reconcile, "to break up a pretence of peaceful unity which is a sham."[32] Hofstadter sums it up concisely: "Our society is sick in many ways; but such health as it has lies in the plurality of the elements composing it and their freedom to interact with each other."[33]

What is true at the community level is also true at the personal level. The goal for wholeness must be communication and compromise rather than rugged individualism on one side or conformity on the other. In the world of the nineteenth and all earlier centuries, human community was more organic than it is now. The individual was born into communities of preformed ties, relationships, and duties. In our more urban world, we have more freedom, but fewer ready-made channels of friendship and community. "One must select, one must take the initiative to establish relationships, rather than merely inherit them."[34] Ours is a world in which persons seeking wholeness find large scope for the qualities of taking the lead and of accepting others in their diversity for what they are.

The breaking down of barriers that should be the proximate goal of ageric man also involves inevitably those worst fractures where both inhumanity and the enmity of nature have brought suffering. Duke, a character in Warren Miller's novel of Harlem, *The Cool World*, speaks out of such a situation, where both injustice and physical disadvantage have cut off and isolated a sector of humanity:[35]

> I rather be dead . . . than work my life out haulin garbage cans or breathin steam in a laundry in the Bronx like my Mother. We dyin all the time but when you get you hand in the pie you live to be old like them white hair women on Park Avenue they walk with canes but they still alive. Unless some body cut you down while he tryen to get his. Well Man that the chance you take. You don't want to take the chance why you live in the cellar. Carry the garbage cans an fight the rats till you dead.

Fulfillment is more, eschatologically speaking, than Duke says it is; but for him, it has to begin by climbing out of the cellar and getting his hand in the pie. Duke's plight and that of his fellows must also be set within the field of vision of ageric man to shatter his pretense and to prompt him into initiative.

"It should by now be clear," says Crane Brinton toward the end of his *The Anatomy of Revolution*, "that it takes almost as many kinds of men and women to make a revolution as to make a world."[36] In history, wholeness will continue to take the form of growing possibilities for communication among men and between groups. The groups themselves will benefit by accessions of unity here and there, but only in the Kingdom of God will the groups and nations become one. In the meantime our goal is to communicate across barriers by initiative in behalf of the human pilgrimage. The symbol of the Kingdom of God, it is true, promises fuller wholeness. We should listen to such students of evolution as Teilhard de Chardin. "After all," he says, "half a million years, perhaps even a million, were required for life to pass from the prehominids to modern man. Should we now start wringing our hands because, less than two centuries after glimpsing a higher state, modern man is still at loggerheads with himself?"[37]

We have commented on the under-achievement, lack of initiative in time and space, of ageric man, but we have not presented any counsel for his worst condition—that sin of pretense. Here we can recommend only the increasing application of criticism: self-criticism, first, of the kind America has demonstrated in good years, such as the time when Senator Robert LaFollette's Progressive Republicans were heard in political circles; or the kind England heard from the Levellers; or the kind the Church heard from Luther. Self-criticism may strip away some of the illusions, but the only sovereign remedy for human pretensions, in the final analysis, is that sense of judgment—and restoration— that comes, as the Reformers had it, from an apprehension of "the glory of God." Ageric man, both in America and in the world at large, will finally know wholeness only from a sense of divinity expressed in every right human act.

NOTES

1. *Church Dogmatics*, I/2, 875, 882.
2. *Ethics*, p. 57; above, p. 74.
3. *Church Dogmatics*, III/2, 166.
4. Let us note that these two symbols came originally from our analysis of reality into the aspects of space and time in Part Four, pp. 149–150, above. The Kingdom of God was the eschatological "spatial" symbol, and the Day of the Lord was the eschatological "temporal" symbol. (As to the former, it is often pointed out that the New Testament thinks of this symbol not in geographical terms, and that "Kingship of God" would be a better rendering of the Greek. We consider that we are safeguarding this concern by thinking of the Kingdom of God as *theonomous space*, and that "spatial" symbol that surpasses all space.) Just as parallel lines meet at infinity, it must be observed that the aspects of finitude we employ, time and space, converge in eschatology; yet there is a certain appropriateness in the spatial

and temporal origins of these two symbols for the end. The Kingdom of God denotes fullness, arrival at realization, the transformation of calling and commonwealth. The Day of the Lord suggests, rather, that we have not realized wholeness, and that not even by running out to meet it, will we ever know complete wholeness in time; at the end of time there will still be judgment. But there will also be restoration, and both symbols converge to this conclusion.

5. Paul Tillich, *Love, Power, and Justice* (New York: University of Oxford Press, Galaxy Books, 1954), p. 114.

6. Above, p. 38.

7. Aquinas: "Every action has goodness in so far as it has being" (*Summa Theologica*, I-II, q. 18, art. 1, p. 522). "The first of created things is being" (*Ibid.*, I, q. 5, art. 2, p. 36). Tillich: "Ontological concepts are a priori in the strict sense of the word." (*Systematic Theology*, I, p. 166).

8. "If we could think away the co-existence with an Other, but otherwise think ourselves as we are," says Schleiermacher, "self-consciousness could then express only activity . . . which, not being directed to any object, would be merely an urge outwards, an indefinite 'agility' without form or color." (*The Christian Faith*, p. 13).

9. *Church Dogmatics*, III/2, 211, 214.

10. Martin Heidegger, *Being and Time* (New York: Harper & Row, 1962), p. 97; Reinhold Niebuhr, *The Nature and Destiny of Man*, I, 204, 212.

11. E. C. Blackman, "Sanctification," *Interpreter's Dictionary* (New York: Abingdon Press, 1962), IV, 210.

12. W. A. Whitehouse, "The Modern Discussion of Eschatology," in William Manson et al., *Eschatology* (Edinburgh: Oliver and Boyd, 1953?), p. 74.

13. Jones, *The Concept of Holiness*, p. 89; above, p. 56.

14. *Sermons on Several Occasions* (*"Forty-Four Sermons"*) (London: Epworth Press, 1944), p. 523.

15. *Ibid.*, pp. 248-49.

16. *The Phenomenon of Man*, p. 262.

17. O. E. Evans, "Kingdom of God," in *Interpreter's Dictionary*, III, 23.

18. *The Phenomenon of Man*, p. 276. But what of the New Testament claim that "flesh and blood" cannot inherit the Kingdom of God? (I Corinthians 15:50) For an ethics based on a monopolar conception of reality, flesh and blood are the only proper inheritors of the Kingdom of God. Yet, the biblical teaching is true in three ways: (1) Men now living, and indeed men living at any given moment in history, will not enter into a realm of life in which there are no more fractures between God and man, man and man, man and nature. Yet all the while this Kingdom will be on the way in real, tangible advances toward wholeness—as, for example, over the period from 1000 to 2000 A.D. when a new vision of the human personality dawned in the Western world. (2) Part of the way to unfracturedness for the individual apparently lies in death. In our personal lives we live toward wholeness; in death we at least re-enter upon wholeness in a return to nature ("dust to dust"), and according to the biblical view of man, we may enter into some unbroken relation with God and the saints. But about the latter, a monopolar view of reality simply maintains a respectful silence. (At the very least, however, we can say that the artificial preservation of bodies current in American funeral practice violates the spirit of the

doctrine that flesh and blood will not see the Kingdom, and attempts, moreover, to prevent the return of the body to the dust that furnished it.) (3) The kind of men we now are does not represent the kind of man who will act at the end of history, and in a decisive crisis inaugurate a new history, as much beyond ours as ours is beyond, say, *Zinjanthropus*. Our flesh and blood cannot be naively extrapolated into the future as representative of what men and human wholeness will be at the end.

19. See the discussion of under-achievement in a preceding chapter, pp. 183–185.

20. H. A. Guy, *The New Testament Doctrine of the 'Last Things'* (London: Oxford University Press, 1948), p. 8.

21. Rudolf Bultmann, *History and Eschatology: the Presence of Eternity* (New York: Harper & Brothers, Harper Torchbooks, 1957), pp. 143-54, 155.

22. *Interpreter's Dictionary*, IV, 181.

23. William Manson, "Eschatology in the New Testament," in Manson et al., *Eschatology*, p. 15.

24. Paul Althaus, *Die letzten Dinge: Lehrbuch der Eschatologie* (Gütersloh: Carl Bertelsmann Verlag, 1957), pp. 359, 361, 362-64.

25. Cf. E. Jenni, "Day of the Lord," *Interpreter's 'Dictionary*, I, 784-85.

26. Brunner, *Christianity and Civilisation*, I, 133.

27. *The Phenomenon of Man*, p. 261.

28. *Advertisements for Myself* (New York: G. P. Putnam's Sons, 1959), p. 388.

29. *Forbes*, July 15, 1964, p. 7.

30. *Anti-Intellectualism in America*, pp. 118-119.

31. *The Religious Factor*, pp. 364-66.

32. *God and the Rich Society*, pp. 5, 116, 131.

33. *Anti-Intellectualism in America*, p. 430.

34. Chad Walsh, "A Hope for Literature," in *The Climate of Faith in Modern Literature*, ed. Nathan A. Scott, Jr. (Greenwich, Conn.: The Seabury Press, 1964), p. 228.

35. Warren Miller, *The Cool World* (Greenwich, Conn.: Fawcett Publications, Crest Reprints, 1964), p. 88.

36. Crane Brinton, *The Anatomy of Revolution* (New York: Prentice Hall, 1952, rev. ed.), p. 132.

37. *The Phenomenon of Man*, p. 255. The *eschaton* is no more some remotely future "stopping point" than "infinity," properly speaking, is some vast number. We may expect the *culmination* of the present stage of history, or even of history as we know it, since in some future age man may have evolved so much from his present condition that we cannot posit a univocity of man in that new age with man in our own. But the human pageant will go on. Just as "infinity" is for the physical scientist a quality of endlessness rather than some monstrous integer, so the *eschaton* should be to the ethicist a quality of openness to man's pilgrimage to wholeness rather than some *terminus ad quem* of history.

INDEX

Action, 21, 119–171
  as context of reality, 121–127
  demonstration (movement), 132
  ethics and conventional theism, 135–145
  implementation (movement), 130–131
  the inadequacy of, 180–186
  the interconvertibility of stance and, 127–133
  knowledge as, 122
  as *koinonia*, 133–134
  operating concepts for fulfillment, 146–166
  realization as end of, 175–186
  Western culture and, 123–124
Activism, 41, 44
  Gospel and, 120
Agape, 33, 163, 164–165
Ageric culture, 46
Alaskan earthquake (1964), 129
Althaus, Paul, 193–194
Altizer, Thomas J. J., 9, 10
Anabaptists, 87
Anatomy of Revolution, The (Brinton), 201
Aquinas, Saint Thomas, 140, 182
Aristotle, 121, 146, 147
Arminius, Jacobus, 19
Augustine, Saint, 13, 14, 19, 33
Automation, 124–125

Bacon, Francis, 80
Bailey, D. S., 78
Baptists, 90
  on faith, 41–42

  reliance on the Bible, 94
  world-denying tendency of, 49
Barmen Declaration, 102
Barth, Karl, 8, 9–10, 11, 14, 17, 37, 39, 45, 49, 57, 60, 76, 104, 155, 156, 186
  on action, 137–138
  on Jesus' act for others, 184
  on *koinonia*, 134
  middle axiom approach of, 143–144
  on natural theology, 139
  sola scriptura of, 90–91
  on the soul, 151
  on transcendence, 136
Basic Christian Ethics (Ramsey), 12
Bennett, John, 78, 131, 143
Berger, Peter L., 72
Bill of Rights, 64
Birmingham (cruiser), war diary of, 132
Bonaventura, Father, 61
Bonhoeffer, Dietrich, 10, 11, 40–41, 74, 155, 156
  on compromise, 159–160
  on realization, 176–177
Boorstin, Daniel J., 15
Boyle, Robert H., 123
Brinton, Crane, 201
Brunner, Emil, 8, 18, 32, 76, 142, 154–156
  on the calling, 151
  on faith, 33
Buber, Martin, 58, 153
Bullock, Alan, 5
Bultmann, Rudolf, 192–193
Burlamqui, 140